The ABCs of Cold War History

The ABCs of Cold War History

Anglo-America, Bloc *Sovietique*, China, 1919–1994

Bruce A. Elleman

William V. Pratt Professor of International History

U.S. Naval War College

Retired

(FHB) | FIRST HILL BOOKS

FIRST HILL BOOKS
An imprint of Wimbledon Publishing Company
www.anthempress.com

This edition first published in UK and USA 2025
by FIRST HILL BOOKS
75–76 Blackfriars Road, London SE1 8HA, UK
or PO Box 9779, London SW19 7ZG, UK
and
244 Madison Ave #116, New York, NY 10016, USA

British Library Cataloguing-in-Publication Data
A catalogue record for this book is available from the British Library.

Library of Congress Cataloging-in-Publication Data: 2024942531
A catalog record for this book has been requested.

ISBN-13: 978-1-83999-227-8 (Pbk)
ISBN-10: 1-83999-227-1 (Pbk)

Cover Credit: South China Morning Post (SCMP); Author Craig Stephens.

This title is also available as an e-book.

In Honor of the World's Best Mother

CONTENTS

INTRODUCTION: THE 75-YEAR COLD WAR IN PERSPECTIVE

This book presents a brief 75-year-long history of the Cold War, 1919–1994, plus its significance today. The Cold War pitted the Anglo-American sea powers against the Soviet continental bloc, with China as the ultimate prize. After World War II, Western Europe was firmly in the Anglo-American camp, as represented by the North Atlantic Treaty Organization (NATO). But from 1972 onward, Washington also used improving diplomatic relations with Beijing to exert extreme military and economic pressure on Moscow from both West and East. This two-pronged pincer resulted in the end of the Cold War on Western, not Soviet, terms: by 1994, the last Russian troops had withdrawn from Germany, marking the true end of the Cold War.

* * *

Chapter A will examine the creation of the Anglo-American special relationship based on their status as sea powers, their cooperation during World War I, the 1919 Versailles Peace Treaty, the revolutionary turmoil in China during the 1920s, and the critical American decision in 1926 to back down and not fight Communism in China.

Chapter B will examine the impact of the 1917 Bolshevik Revolution and especially the 1919 founding of the Communist International (Comintern), the 1924 creation of the continental Soviet bloc, the 1929 Sino-Soviet War, the tumultuous 1930s, World War II, the diplomatic treaties ending the war, plus Soviet competition with America and England from 1945 to 1949 to dominate China.

Chapter C will discuss a China torn between the Anglo-American-led sea powers and the Soviet-led continental powers, ultimately joining the Soviet bloc in 1949. The American sea power strategy to win Cold War I was to push Beijing and Moscow closer together so as to break up the Sino-Soviet alliance, to arm China—both militarily and economically—and then to use China's rapidly developing sea power to undermine the continental Union of Soviet Socialist Republics (USSR) from both the West with NATO and the East with China. Soon after the 1960 Sino-Soviet split, and especially after the 1969 Sino-Soviet war, China renounced the USSR, opened talks with Richard Nixon in 1972, and rejoined the West in 1979, when it left the Soviet bloc forever. Thereafter, China cooperated with the sea powers to end the Cold War and destroy the Soviet Union.

In the Conclusion, the Cold War's historical impact and strategic significance will be discussed, highlighting how continental-minded Vladimir Putin and Xi Jinping once again appear to be combining against the Anglo-American-led sea powers. Will history "rhyme," as Mark Twain said, and will the Anglo-American West win Cold War II, or will events turn out very differently this time?

*   *   *

The *ABCs of Cold War History: Anglo-America, Bloc Sovietique, China, 1919–1994* provides an Eurasian-centric history of the U.S. Cold War policies with the USSR and China. Beginning in 1972 and continuing throughout the 1980s, China imported critical high technology from the United States and the United Kingdom, particularly to develop the PLA Navy (PLAN). Western technology also helped jumpstart China's economy. This growing Chinese military and economic threat created huge effects on the USSR.

When the Soviet leader Mikhail Gorbachev tried to replicate China's enormous growth rates, he failed, resulting in the end of the Cold War and the USSR's collapse. With the end of the Cold War, the Soviet Navy was eliminated almost overnight as the world's second-most powerful navy; Russia's Pacific fleet was so poorly supplied and equipped that it would rarely leave port.

This unprecedented reversal of Russia's fortunes created a maritime vacuum that China has been trying to fill ever since. In recent years, former Sino-U.S. cooperation has changed more and more to competition, as a rising China has sparked increased tensions in the South China Sea and elsewhere.

*   *   *

This history will conclude by reexamining contemporary Sino-Russian cooperation and tensions. Specifically, can China and Russia overcome their historic animosity and traditional rivalry to work together effectively against the United States, the United Kingdom, and their many sea power allies? Some commentators are even calling this tense relationship a second Cold War. If so, which continental factors might support deeper cooperation between the People's Republic of China (PRC) and Russia, and conversely, which sea power factors might undermine it? Will the Anglo-American-led sea powers be able to win Cold War II like they won Cold War I?

Chapter A

THE ANGLO-AMERICAN
SPECIAL RELATIONSHIP

The British island location made becoming a sea power a necessity, but the United States made a conscious decision to adopt sea power. In 1890, naval theorist Alfred Thayer Mahan published his classic *The Influence of Sea Power upon History*, laying out six prerequisites for sea powers: (1) secure borders provided by an oceanic moat in combination with nonexistent landward threats; (2) a dense internal transportation grid; (3) reliable egress by sea precluding blockade in wartime; (4) a dense coastal population; (5) a commerce-driven economy; and (6) stable government institutions promoting both commerce and a consistent foreign policy.[1] The United Kingdom was naturally a sea power, but the United States consciously became one when it adopted a large navy but retained a small army. In 1904, the two countries cemented their "special relationship," which has now lasted for over 120 years. The Anglo-American "special relationship" played an essential role in the Cold War.

* * *

America was created facing the Atlantic Ocean, but by 1898 it had also become a Pacific power. The Pacific Ocean has three major North-South island chains, including the so-called "first island chain" that runs from the tip of the Kamchatka Peninsula down through the Kurile Islands, the Japanese home islands, Okinawa, Taiwan, and on through to the Philippines. The so-called "second island chain" splits away from Japan and runs southward toward the Bonins, Guam, and the Marshall Islands. Meanwhile, the so-called "third island chain" runs from the end of the Aleutian Trench southward along the Emperor Seamount, through Midway, and ends up in the Hawaiian Islands. (See Map 1.)

---

1 Alfred Thayer Mahan, *The Influence of Sea Power upon History 1660–1783* (1890; repr. New York: Wang and Hill, 1957), 481.

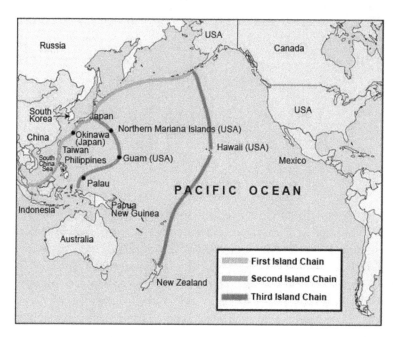

Map 1 The three island chains.

Japan was also a rising sea power that soon challenged the United States. During the late nineteenth century, Japan expanded along the first and second island chains and into the Western Pacific. In 1876, Japan obtained all of the Kurile Islands in exchange for ceding the southern half of Sakhalin Island to Russia and also seized the Bonin Islands, about 1,000 miles to the southeast of Japan. In 1879, the Ryukyu Islands were formally annexed by Japan and became the prefecture of Okinawa. Finally, after the First Sino-Japanese War (1894–1895), Japan obtained the island of Taiwan—in theory in perpetuity—in 1895, which gave it unbroken control from Kamchatka to Taiwan. This gave Japan strategic leverage over all of its neighbors, in particular China.

Washington saw Tokyo's expansion as a threat since it effectively cut the U.S. sea line of communication to China. In 1897, assistant secretary of the Navy, Theodore Roosevelt, and Commander C. J. Goodrich, president of the U.S. Naval War College (NWC), carried on a confidential correspondence discussing how Japan's recent expansion impacted the United States. On June 23, 1897, Goodrich explained that any Japanese attack on the United States would have to be staged from either Dutch Harbor (Unalaska) in the Aleutians or from Hawaii: "Honolulu, on the other hand, is the bone of contention, and therefore a principal objective point. [...] it can be approached by stages, Midway, or one of the adjacent islands being occupied for a base or coaling station whence to operate against Honolulu, only 1000 miles or so distant. Such a course of action by Japan would force the U.S. to operate at a distance of 2000 miles from its own coast." Even if American forces took Hawaii in a U.S.-Japanese war, Tokyo could still "profit by the exceptional facilities for approach afforded her by the scattered islands lying to the westward of the Hawaiian group."[2]

During the very next year, in the midst of the 1898 Spanish-American War, which was nominally being fought over Cuba, Washington used the conflict with Spain as its strategic rationale to annex Hawaii outright and to invade Guam and the Philippines. Through the December 10, 1898, Treaty of Paris, Spain ceded the Philippine Islands to the United States for $20 million, while Guam became a permanent U.S. territory. In a single stroke, Washington consolidated control over strategic bases on the first, second, and third island chains and, in so doing, reopened a direct naval route to China. Arguably, this was the real reason for fighting the war with Spain; Cuba was just a convenient diversion.

By 1898, the U.S. government had consciously acquired naval bases on all three of these island chains. These territorial gains made the United States a Pacific power, which later helped it to win the Pacific War against Japan. Soon after World War II ended, the U.S. government carried through on its previous promises and granted the Philippines independence in 1946. But the United States retained its strategic bases in Hawaii, Guam, and, especially, Okinawa, which still hosts 75 percent of U.S. bases in Japan in terms of area, even though Okinawa represents just 0.6 percent of Japan's total territory. These bases are still the foundation of American sea power in the Pacific. Some critics call it hegemonic power.

* * *

Although Great Britain and the United States were in many ways natural sea power allies, it was the Venezuelan Crisis of 1902–1903 that led to the formation of their "special relationship." On December 7, 1902, Germany and Britain instituted a "peaceful blockade" of Venezuela to force it to pay off its overdue foreign debts. But American president Roosevelt opposed this action

---

2 Captain C.F. Goodrich, "Letter to Assistant Secretary on War with Japan," June 23, 1897, XSTP, U.S. Naval War College Historical Archives, 7 pages; cited in Bruce A. Elleman, *The Impact of Coincidence in Modern American, British, and Asian History: Twenty-One Unusual Historical Events* (London: Anthem Press, 2023), 3–6, plus the rest of this short section.

as a violation of the Monroe Doctrine. During the "winter exercises" of 1902–
1903, the U.S. Navy's 53 ships countered the 29 ships available to Britain and
Germany in the Caribbean. War appeared likely. Outnumbered by the U.S.
"fleet-in-being," on December 17, 1902, the two European nations lifted their
naval blockade and agreed to arbitrate the matter with Venezuela instead.[3]

The British decision to back down in the Venezuelan Crisis had another,
albeit unintended, result. The British Colonial Office drafted a secret memorandum acknowledging that the U.S. Navy could "stop our supplies from
Canada," plus halt all American imports, effectively cutting off two-thirds
of Great Britain's food supply. This potential threat emphasized "the necessity of preserving good relations with the United States."[4] Within two years,
John Balfour and Lord Lansdowne would secure an unofficial security
arrangement with America, the beginning of what has come to be known as
a "Special Relationship" that has lasted ever since, for well over a century.[5]
Post-World War I, these two sea power nations, plus their allies, represented
one side of the evolving Cold War.

Meanwhile, the Soviet bloc represented the other side of the Cold War. In
1904, Halford J. Mackinder published an article entitled "The Geographical
Pivot of History," arguing that continental countries like Russia had an
important geographical advantage over sea powers. Their central location
allowed them to pivot effortlessly from one front to another, giving them an
important edge during wars. (See Map 2.) Unlike free trade espoused by sea
powers, however, land powers created "spheres of influence," or "spheres of
interest," which they could dominate both economically and politically. The
difference between "free trade" and "spheres of influence" was at the heart
of the Cold War.

* * *

One of the most important joint Anglo-American goals was to open up
China to free trade under the "Open Door Policy," to modernize China in

---

3 Henry J. Hendrix, "Overwhelming Force and the Venezuelan Crisis of 1902-1903," in
   Bruce A. Elleman and S.C.M. Paine, Eds., *Navies and Soft Power: Historical Case Studies of
   Naval Power and the Nonuse of Military Force* (Newport, RI: NWC Press, 2015), 21. Much
   of the description of the Venezuelan Crisis is based on this chapter.
4 Ibid., citing "Caribbean Sea and Western Atlantic: Strategic Conditions in Event of
   War with the United States," January 21, 1903, Admiralty Group (ADM) 1/8875,
   TNA/UK.
5 Ibid., citing William N. Tilchin, *Theodore Roosevelt and the British Empire: A Study in
   Presidential Statecraft* (New York: St. Martin's Press, 1997), 102–105.

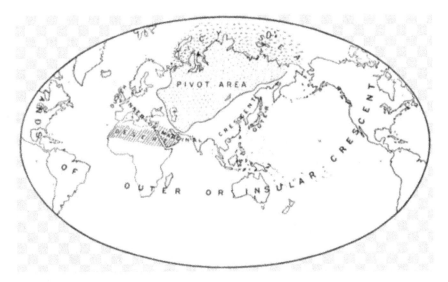

Map 2 The geographical pivot of history.

line with Western principles, and to support China's gradual adoption of international law and democracy. With Britain's backing, Washington supported the Open Door Policy beginning in 1899, forcing the other foreign powers to promise not to divide up China into competing spheres of influence. However, this goal was undermined by General Yuan Shikai, a high military official of the Qing Dynasty who turned against the Manchus in 1912, succeeded Sun Yat-sen as democratic China's first leader, and then attempted to found a new imperial dynasty by signing treaties with Japan and Tsarist Russia in 1915.

Although retired from the Qing Army, when the Double Ten (10 October) Revolution began in 1911, the Manchus summoned General Yuan back to duty. However, Yuan was in no rush, and he agreed to take on the command of the army only after being made China's prime minister. Yuan then entered into negotiations with the revolutionaries, and he played the Qing court off the politically inexperienced Nationalist leader Sun Yat-sen. By March 1912, the Manchus had abdicated, and Yuan was named president of the Republic of China.

Over the next two years, Yuan Shikai engaged in political intrigue, subverting the democratic government. After destroying the revolutionaries' political and military authority, Yuan dissolved the National Assembly, replacing it with a political council composed of his own cronies. The 1914 outbreak of World War I presented Yuan with new difficulties, plus great opportunities. As Western interest shifted away from East Asia, the Japanese were given a relatively free hand. As an ally of Great Britain, Japan seized the German territorial concessions in Qingdao, Shandong, thereby destroying the last German foothold in the Far East.

During January 1915, the Japanese presented Yuan with 21 Demands, including virtually total Japanese control over China's finances, police, and many other government affairs. If all 21 demands had been granted as written, China would have been transformed into little more than a Japanese protectorate. This was contrary to American and British interests. But they were busy fighting in Europe, so no foreign power intervened militarily to stop Japan. As a result, Yuan submitted to all but the most radical of these 21 demands. Yuan was simultaneously dealing secretly with Tsarist Russian officials. In 1915, Beijing and Moscow agreed to a tripartite pact, turning Outer Mongolia into a puppet state under Russian protection. In violation of the Open Door Policy, Russia secretly added this huge chunk of Chinese territory to its "sphere of influence."

Sun Yat-sen claimed that Yuan actually proposed these 21 demands in return for Tokyo's support in recognizing him as the new emperor of China. In a 1917 publication, Sun said: "In fact, the Twenty-one Demands were presented by Japan at his own instigation: Japan did not, in the beginning, press him to accept these demands."[6] On November 12, 1917, U.S. ambassador to China W. G. Sharp confirmed this story when he reported to President Woodrow Wilson that the Japanese "ultimatum" was merely a ploy to appease the Japanese people. In fact, only those demands acceptable to China were called an "ultimatum." This charade allowed Yuan to "keep face" by blaming Japan for forcing concessions even while obtaining Japan's support to become China's new emperor.[7] (Document 1)

Yuan's desire to found a new imperial dynasty moved forward with Japan's and Tsarist Russia's backing. By December 1915, his supporters had petitioned him to found a new dynasty. Government orders were then issued, transforming China from a republic back to a monarchy. Unfortunately for Yuan, this was met with widespread domestic resistance. By March 1916, his coup was over, and Yuan reluctantly restored the Chinese republican government. Throughout the spring, Yuan tried but failed to negotiate a settlement with the rebel military commanders. In June 1916, exhausted and ill, Yuan died of kidney disease. China narrowly retained its democratic government.

---

6 Elleman, *The Impact of Coincidence*, 11–14, citing Sun Yat-sen, *The Vital Problems of China* (Taipei: China Cultural Service, 1953 reprint), 55.
7 Bruce A. Elleman, *Wilson and China: A Revised History of the Shandong Question* (Armonk, NY: M.E. Sharpe, 2002), 19.

PARIS, November 14, 1917

My dear Mr. President:

In my letter of some little time ago, after having dwelt upon conditions then prevailing in France, I promised to write you giving my observations concerning some of the problems confronting the Allies having to do with their relations toward each other.

Mr. Koo Jai Teh said that he strongly believed it was Japanese intrigue that later fomented the disturbances in Southern China, with the object of furnishing an excuse for Japan to come in and establish order. He narrated in an amusing manner an interesting story of how, to appease the people of Japan, that Government had given out for home consumption the fact that an ultimatum had been given to China imposing certain conditions upon her which she would be compelled to accept. As a matter of fact, a considerable number of the original provisions of the ultimatum had been refused by China and others compatible to her dignity and security had been accepted. Those that had been accepted were proudly announced in Tokio as being the ultimatum to which Japan was soon going to force China to agree. A further phase of this international game lay in the fact that, while it had been solemnly enjoined upon the Chinese Government not to make known any of the rejected Articles of the so-called ultimatum which had been proposed, yet the British and other Governments at Pekin had been let into the "secret", that only the accepted provisions had been proposed to China.

As I am despatching this letter, I am reminded by its date that it should reach you on the eve of the day when the fine sentiments expressed in your Thanksgiving Day proclamation will be read from a number of the public places in Paris.

Believe me, dear Mr. President,

Very sincerely yours,

W. G. Sharp

Document 1 U.S. Ambassador to China W. G. Sharp's 14 November 1917 Letter to President Woodrow Wilson.

*   *   *

Even though Yuan Shikai failed to become China's new emperor, Japan kept its diplomatic gains, as did Russia. China would later try, and fail, to cancel the 21 Demands at the 1919 Paris Peace Conference, where Wilson was unfairly blamed for betraying China. Wilson's "secret" compromise resolving the Sino-Japanese Shandong question divided the problem into "political" versus "economic" issues. Wilson succeeded at convincing Japan to reverse all negative political terms of the 21 Demands, thereby protecting China's political interests. However, Japan was ceded Shandong by Germany and then promised to return it to China, the so-called indirect resolution, versus Germany returning its concession directly to China.

Wilson negotiated this compromise with the Japanese delegation during the last week of April 1919. After careful deliberation, the Japanese acquiesced, and on April 30, 1919, they agreed to retain economic rights in Shandong but no military or political rights. This solution protected Chinese sovereignty, plus completely avoided referring back to, and thereby recognizing, the 21 Demands plus later treaties from 1918 that had infringed on China. In effect, Wilson convinced Japan to wipe the slate clean and build all future Sino-Japanese diplomatic relations on the basis of equality and goodwill.

But Wilson's personal secretary back in Washington neglected to release this agreement. Tumulty wrote, "I will therefore do nothing about the Japanese matter unless you insist."[8] (Document 2) Because Wilson's agreement was not widely publicized, most Chinese did not realize a compromise with Japan had been struck, one that ultimately gave China back Shandong. The student demonstrations of May 4, 1919, were to turn China irrevocably away from Wilson and the West and toward socialism and eventually Communism. When the Chinese Communist Party (CCP) was founded in July 1921, it was in part a reaction to a widespread belief that China had "lost face" because Shandong was not returned directly by Germany.

These murky diplomatic events in Paris opened the door for greater Soviet influence in China. The July 25, 1919, Karakhan Manifesto promised to cede to China all of the rights and privileges that the Versailles Treaty had appeared to refuse. Soon after the 1917 October Revolution (November 7, 1917, by the Western Calendar) succeeded, a major Bolshevik foreign policy strategy was to form alliances with Asian democrats to draw them into a global "United Front" against capitalism. China's revolutionary leader Sun Yat-sen was high on the Bolshevik list as a possible ally. The Communists became a rapidly growing force within China after 1921, and by the late 1940s, the CCP took power throughout Mainland China.

*   *   *

To put the Bolsheviks' actions in China into a broader context, on February 22, 1919, an article in *Izvestiia* explained Vladimir Lenin's 1913 two-camp

---

8 Ibid., citing the Japanese Foreign Ministry Archives (Gaimushō), File: 2.3.1-3.4.

The White House,
Washington.

CODE

1 May, 1919.

The President of the United States,

Paris.

I have not made use of the Japanese statement, but am keeping my ear
to the ground and waiting. My feeling is that an attempt to explain
the compromise, when no demand is made, would weaken our position
instead of strengthening it. I will therefore do nothing about the
Japanese matter unless you insist. It would help if I could unof-
ficially say: First. The date of your probable return to the country;
Second. Whether tour country to discuss the League of Nations is possible.
The adoption of the labor program as part of the peace program, is most
important, but not enough emphasis is being placed upon it. Could you
not make a statement of some kind that we could use here, showing the importance of this program as helping toward the stabilization of labor
conditions throughout 'the world.

20633   TUMULTY.

Document 2 Wilson's Personal Secretary Tumulty Refused to Release the Secret Agreement.

division of the world into two "irreconcilable camps." The Bolsheviks defined all capitalist, bourgeois-democratic countries as imperialist, thus splitting the global struggle between "the camp of imperialism and the camp of socialism." In the imperialist camp were the "United States, Britain, France, and Japan," while the socialist camp contained "Soviet Russia with the young soviet republics, and the growing proletariat revolution in the European countries." *Izvestiia* predicted that the "roar" of the socialist revolutions could already be "heard in the countries of the oppressed East."[9] The USSR's December 30, 1922, constitution canonized this Cold War schism: "The world has been divided into two camps—the capitalist and the socialist."[10] After World War II, the Soviet ideologue, Andrei Zhdanov, repeated this "two-camp" thesis during 1947, just as Khrushchev would preach the "victory of socialism over capitalism."[11]

Clearly, the Cold War had already begun in East Asia by 1919, as China was urged by the Bolsheviks to join the socialist camp. Soon afterwards, during March 1919, the formation of the Comintern repeated this claim. In fact, one of the two Chinese delegates, Lao Xiuzhao, published an article in *Izvestiia* arguing that 500 million Chinese were being exploited by the capitalist powers of Europe, America, and Japan under the guise of America's Open Door Policy. To oppose this exploitation, Lao even named the Chinese leader with whom the Comintern hoped to ally, the "pride of China—Sun Yat-sen."[12]

China was the biggest prize in the Cold War. The Soviet government and the Comintern actively sought to ally with Sun Yat-sen's government in South China. This was confirmed during the summer of 1919 in a propaganda pamphlet written by a Soviet government official, Vladimir Vilenskii. This pamphlet cited the Karakhan Manifesto when it explained that the Bolsheviks were very interested in Sun's revolutionary movement in South China because: "Everyone is saying that the revolutionary fire in South China ought inevitably to move to the North. Then revolutionary Russia will find for itself a reliable ally in China against the imperialist predators."[13]

These Soviet declarations were the first signs of what would soon become an important Cold War foreign policy strategy: actively promoting colonial revolutions in Asia and throughout the Third World by organizing, training, and funding so-called "native revolutionaries."[14] The Bolsheviks hoped that Sun Yat-sen would prove to be one of the Bolsheviks' most important allies.

---

9 Xenia Joukoff Eudin and Robert C. North, *Soviet Russia and the East, 1920-1927* (Stanford, CA: Stanford University Press, 1957), 45–46.

10 Official English-language copy of "The Fundamental Law (Constitution) of the Union of Socialist Soviet Republics," Nangang, Taiwan, Wai Jiao Dang An (WJDA), 03-32, 461(3).

11 William Hyland, *The Cold War is Over* (New York: Random House, 1990), 7.

12 "Predstavitel' Kitaia o III Internatsionale" (*The Chinese Representative about the Third International*), *Izvestiia*, March 6, 1919.

13 Vladimir Vilenskii, *Kitai i Sovetskaia Rossiia (China and Soviet Russia)* (Moscow: Gosudarstvennoe izdatel'stvo, 1919), 3, 12.

14 "Komintern na Vostoke" ("The Comintern in the East"), *Kommunisticheskii Internatsional (Communist International)*, No. 9–10 (1929), 20.

Although Comintern representatives would later hold talks with many other influential Chinese revolutionaries, these early attempts to contact Sun's separatist Guangzhou government show that he was highly considered.[15]

The Soviet goal was to turn Guangzhou against Beijing. After all, Sun Yat-sen was one of the primary political opponents of Russia's traditional adversary, Beijing, and the enemy of my enemy is my friend. During early diplomatic talks in Beijing, Soviet envoys promised to abolish publicly all the former unequal treaties, but only if Beijing officials secretly agreed to retain the unequal terms. This ploy was, in fact, just another way of retaining all of Tsarist Russia's special rights and privileges in China. This was a Bolshevik subterfuge that Beijing officials refused to accept. Moscow needed Sun's support to make Beijing agree to this unequal relationship.

* * *

The U.S. government convened the Washington Conference during 1921–1922 to resolve many outstanding Asian problems, including a timetable for the Shandong concession's return to China, which took place on December 10, 1922. During October and November 1920, the British Foreign Office had to choose between the United States and Japan and felt compelled to side with America: "If the cardinal feature of our foreign policy in the future is to cultivate closer relations with the United States [...] the renewal of the alliance [with Japan] in anything like its present shape may prove a formidable obstacle to the realization of that aim." In line with its decision, Britain backed the Open Door Policy's support for the "independence and integrity of China." The shift from a bilateral alliance with Japan to a four-way alliance including Britain, Japan, the United States, and France was portrayed as "a constructive policy for the rehabilitation of China."[16]

By the early 1920s, all of the Bolshevik-backed proletarian revolutions in Europe had failed. Moscow had no choice but to support revolutions in colonial and semi-colonial nations. The Bolsheviks' ultimate goal was to destroy the underpinnings of the international capitalist system. The

---

15 The Comintern also sent the Dutch agent Maring to China to visit the Guangzhou warlord Chen Jiongming on three different occasions to discuss forming an alliance with him, proving that geography actually mattered more than personalities. Historical Commission of the Central Committee of the Guomindang Party - Contemporary History collection: 467 - 39, 15; Chou Fuo-hai, *A Report of a Flight from the Red Capital Wuhan* (1927), 1, 7–8.

16 Richard Stremski, *Britain's China Policy, 1920-1928* (University of Wisconsin Dissertation, 1968), 21–22.

1923 United Front between the CCP and Sun Yat-sen's Nationalist Party was a prime example. The Comintern broke 1919–1929 into two five-year periods: the first characterized "primarily by open battles of the proletariat in the European capitalist countries," and the second by "the development of waves of revolutionary insurrections and battles of the colonial peoples."[17]

By 1924, Moscow had leveraged the United Front to renew its unequal treaties with Beijing. A secret protocol attached to the May 31, 1924 Sino-Soviet Friendship Treaty agreed that all former unequal treaties were recognized but not enforced (Document 3). So long as new treaties were never negotiated, however, Moscow argued that the former treaties' unequal terms remained valid. Simply by refusing to discuss a new treaty, therefore, the Bolsheviks claimed the old treaty terms still existed. This loophole remained a highly guarded secret, since Beijing officials would "lose face" by admitting they had been duped. When other foreign governments hesitated to give up their own special rights and privileges, Beijing supported the myth of Sino-Soviet equality to undermine them. The imperialist powers were thus put under extreme pressure to give up their own special rights in China.

*   *   *

During spring 1925, the USSR was in a good position to use its recently acquired status as the only power claiming to treat China as an equal to undermine and destroy the United States' and Great Britain's political, legal, and cultural positions in China. For the first time, the Bolsheviks acknowledged that the most important of the colonial revolutions was to be found in China.[18] During May 1925, with the revolutionary wave in China on the rise, Joseph Stalin announced that the Bolshevik revolution had entered a new stage, the "overthrow of the bourgeoisie on a world scale." He defined the opposing camps as "the camp of capitalism under the leadership of Anglo-American capital, and the camp of socialism under the leadership of the Soviet Union." Stalin set the terms of this two-camp Cold War by announcing that "the international situation will in a greater and greater degree be determined by the relationship of forces between the two camps." If the capitalist countries tried to attack the USSR, it would once again become an

---

17 "Komintern na Vostoke," 20.
18 G. Zinoviev, "Vsemirno-istoricheskoe znachenie shankhaiskikh sobytii" (The Worldwide Historical Significance of the Shanghai Events), *Pravda*, June 7, 1925.

Document 3 Secret Protocol Attached to the 31 May 1924 Sino-Soviet Friendship Treaty.

"impregnable fortress" by calling on its allies, the "workers of the West and the oppressed peoples of the East," to "unleash the revolutionary lion in every country of the world."[19]

---

19 "Extracts from a Report by Stalin on the Work of the Fourteenth Conference of the Communist Party of the Soviet Union," May 9, 1925, Jane Degras, *Soviet Documents on Foreign Policy. Volume 2, 1925-1932* (New York: Oxford University Press, 1952), 25–28.

The revolutionary Chinese also adopted military force. For example, the 1925 May 30th Movement ushered in a two-year period of anti-foreign strikes that included violent attacks on the British concessions in Guangzhou, against the International Settlement in Shanghai, and against foreign enclaves in Hankou, Jiujiang, and Nanjing. Chinese participants in these anti-foreign demonstrations often included military cadets trained by Soviet advisers in China and were in large part organized and sponsored by the Comintern, a Soviet-funded organization.

The Western nations felt directly threatened by the Chinese revolution. Soviet-sponsored propaganda specifically condemned foreign tariff controls as enslaving China. On November 19, 1925, the American, British, and Japanese delegates to a Special Tariff Conference recognized that China should have the right to set higher tariffs on imported goods, and the delegates agreed to grant China tariff autonomy by the year 1929.[20] The Bolsheviks, of course, secretly retained lower tariffs based on Tsarist Russia's unequal treaties. Their goal was to make China part of the Soviet "sphere of influence" and ultimately a full-fledged member of the Soviet bloc.

Faced with a rapidly deteriorating position in China, the British Foreign Office issued a statement on September 30, 1926, warning that Great Britain was prepared to defend its legitimate interests in China "from pirates and robbers who, with their actions, pose a threat to the lives and property of British subjects."[21] The British government tried its best to convince the U.S. government to intervene militarily in China as well, but all of its efforts failed.[22] U.S. secretary of state Frank Kellogg was convinced that the Chinese people's desire for equal treatment was completely legitimate. On November 29, 1926, he telegraphed the American consulate in Beijing, denying their request that the U.S. Navy be used to protect the foreign customs house in Hankou from attack:[23]

> The Chinese Maritime Customs was brought into existence by the Government of China. It is a Chinese national service; it functions under the orders and protection of the Government of China, and the foreigners employed in it are servants of that Government. If that Government

---

20 Akira Iriye, *After Imperialism, The Search for a New Order in the Far East, 1921-1931* (Cambridge, MA: Harvard University Press, 1965), 75.

21 *Daily Telegraph*, September 30, 1926.

22 Roberta Allbert Dayer, *Bankers and Diplomats in China 1917-1925 The Anglo-American Relationship* (London: Frank Cass and Co., 1981), 236.

23 John Carter Vincent, *The Extraterritorial System in China* (Cambridge, MA: Harvard University Press, 1970), 10.

should desire the destruction of the Customs Administration, or if the desire of the Chinese people is to destroy the Government of China and the Customs Administration it has created, the basis of right upon which this Government may intervene in order to prevent either purpose from being accomplished is difficult to see. In consequence, I am unable to see my way clear, in regard to preventing the operation of the Customs house at Hankou from being paralyzed, to authorize landing an armed force in cooperation with other powers.

The Anglo-American special relationship faltered when it came to China. American support for the Nationalist movement in China was just too strong.

During December 1925, the Comintern-funded journal *The Communist International*, reevaluated the respective strengths of the Western powers in China versus the growing influence of the USSR. Great Britain's enormous financial losses due to Hong Kong strikes meant that it was no longer Moscow's main adversary. Instead, E. Varga, a well-known Hungarian Comintern official, announced that the "final struggle between the world bourgeoisie and proletariat will take place under the leadership of the United States and the Union of Socialist Republics."[24] The US-USSR Cold War was now officially on.

* * *

The quarter-century-long Anglo-American special relationship faltered when it came to protecting China from Communism. Instead of fighting Communism there, in China, the U.S. government backed down. Respecting the will of the Chinese people, Washington decided that the only right thing to do was to terminate U.S. policies, even though they were intended to support China. This meant dismantling many of the Open Door Policy's protections for China's sovereignty and national self-determination.

Kellogg's decision not to intervene militarily was based on his belief that the Chinese people were exercising their natural right to rebel against their own government. What he did not know was that the Bolsheviks had resorted to secret diplomacy to retain Tsarist Russia's special rights and concessions. So, Kellogg, like many other foreigners, saw China's revolutionary movement as a Wilsonian-type Nationalist revolution when it was really a Leninist

---

24 E. Varga, "Puti i prepiatstviia mirovoi revoliutsii" (Paths and Obstacles of the World Revolution), *Kommunisticheskii Internatsional* (Communist International), December 1925, #12, 5–23.

anti-imperialist revolution. It was the myth of Sino-Soviet equality that gave legitimacy to the Soviet-backed revolutionary movement in China.

Meanwhile, because its imperialist policies were based on secret diplomacy, the USSR largely escaped criticism for its own expansionist policies, since these policies were carried out in complete secrecy. This included taking control of Outer Mongolia and adding it to the Soviet bloc, plus retaining the Tsarist Russian railway and territorial concessions in Manchuria as Soviet spheres of influence. The Soviet-led revolution in China ultimately failed in 1927, but it was an ironic twist that public demonstrations throughout China unwittingly helped create the Soviet bloc. Furthermore, any diminution of Westerners' sea power leverage in China made them a less effective counterweight to any future Soviet continental expansion.

Chapter B

THE BLOC *SOVIETIQUE* CHALLENGE

After being established by the October 1917 Revolution, the Soviet Union narrowly managed to survive the 1920s and 1930s, persevering in part by tapping formerly unknown gold and petroleum sources in Siberia and Outer Mongolia. Soviet diplomatic maneuvering with Beijing during spring 1924 strengthened the Soviet sphere of influence in Outer Mongolia, allowing Moscow to exploit its gold resources. By fall 1924, Outer Mongolia became the very first Asian member of the "bloc *Sovietique*," or simply the Soviet bloc.[1] Without access to these untapped Asian mineral riches, the Soviet government might have collapsed when the Great Depression hit unexpectedly in 1929.

*   *   *

Based on the unequal terms of the Tsarist Russian 1915 tripartite treaty with Yuan Shikai, the Soviet Army invaded Outer Mongolia in 1921. The Soviets immediately cut off Tannu Tuva, a large portion of Mongolia's north-west corner bigger than the size of Greece, and quickly turned it into a puppet state. While Moscow repeatedly promised Beijing that it would withdraw its troops, during May 1924, the American vice-consul in Kalgan, Edwin F. Stanton, reported that "the present Soviet Government, acting in an advisory capacity to the Mongolian Government, but actually dictating its policies and its administration, does not intend to relinquish either political or economic control of Outer Mongolia."[2] In fact, Moscow's creation of the Soviet bloc to include Outer Mongolia in 1924 was significant, since Outer Mongolia's

---

1 Bruce A. Elleman, *Diplomacy and Deception: The Secret History of Sino-Soviet Diplomatic Relations, 1917-1927* (Armonk, NY: M.E. Sharpe, 1997), 85–113 passim. Citing April 14, 1924, WJDA, 03-32, 510(3).

2 Alicia J. Campi, *The Political Relationship Between the United States and Outer Mongolia, 1915-1927: The Kalgan Consular Records* (Indiana University Dissertation, 1988), 202–203; cited in Elleman, *The Impact of Coincidence*, 31–34, plus following section.

previously untapped gold and mineral resources made it of great strategic and financial importance.

Even while publicly acknowledging that Outer Mongolia was part of China, Moscow sought to retain it secretly. Part of the mystery surrounding Soviet envoy Lev Karakhan's unwillingness to compromise on Outer Mongolia was cleared up on April 14, 1924, when Foreign Minister Wellington Koo received a letter from C. R. Bennett, a representative of an American bank in China, warning him of a new German and Soviet consortium to mine gold in East Asia: "[An] unimpeachable commercial source has reached me to the effect a composite political commercial financial technical group is now under establishment in Moscow and Berlin for the purpose of surveying and considering means of opening up and working all of the Eastern gold and other precious mineral fields of Siberia and particularly as affecting China's interest [...]"[3] Koo further learned that the USSR and Germany were cooperating with each other to exploit gold mines in Outer Mongolia. Documents in the Foreign Ministry Archives in Tokyo show that a councilor to the German Foreign Office named Assmis visited Outer Mongolia during 1922 on behalf of Count Brockdorff-Rantzau. Assmis admitted that he was working with Moscow to determine "Russian and German interest[s] in developing the Far Eastern territories of Russia." Assmis also explained that "the Russian face has turned eastwards again, and the Russians will take up the old [ts]arist imperialist policy against China and Japan," as well as proclaiming that Outer Mongolia "is practically on the way to be[ing] a Russian province."[4]

Koo demanded that Karakhan abolish the Tsarist Russian 1915 tripartite treaty, plus a more recent Soviet-Mongolia treaty from 1921. But this would have interfered with German-Soviet efforts to exploit Outer Mongolia's natural resources, especially gold. The May 31, 1924, Sino-Soviet Treaty agreed that Outer Mongolia was an integral part of China: "The Government of the Union of Soviet Socialist Republics recognizes that Outer Mongolia is an integral part of the Republic of China and respects China's sovereignty therein." But a secret protocol recognized the existence of all former treaties, even though both sides acknowledged they were not to be enforced. Simply by refusing to renegotiate new treaties, therefore, the Soviets retained the unequal treaty terms.

This secret protocol helped the Bolsheviks turn Outer Mongolia into a Soviet protectorate. Soon after the death of the Bogdo Khan, the so-called

---

3 English-language letter from C.R. Bennett to Wellington Koo, April 14, 1924, WJDA, 03-32, 510(3).

4 Gaimushō, File 2.5.1.106-1. Document # 437.

"Living Buddha," on May 20, 1924, all lamas between 18 and 30 years old were drafted into the Mongolian army. This ended virtually all organized religious opposition to becoming a Soviet protectorate. Soon afterwards, American, European, and Japanese businessmen were arrested and detained, reportedly as part of a purge within the Revolutionary Youth League, an organization "entirely dominated by Soviet Advisers and more particularly the head of the Secret Police."[5] By September 14, 1924, all foreigners were kicked out, and the Soviet Union's "sphere of influence" in Outer Mongolia was now complete.

The purge then underway also had important political ramifications. On November 25, 1924, Outer Mongolia adopted a new constitution, changed its official name to the Mongolian People's Republic, and renamed the capital Urga to Ulaan Bataar. This purge allowed the Mongolian secret police to pave "the way for the complete Sovietization of Outer Mongolia."[6] Relations between Moscow and Ulaan Bataar soon became so close that, in 1925, "Stalinist restrictions, controls, and political radicalization unfolded in Mongolia with seeming inevitability, just as they were developing in the Soviet Union itself."[7]

In 1924, Outer Mongolia became the very first Asian member of the Soviet bloc. During the early 1920s, the Bolsheviks opened the Nalaikh gold mine 20 miles from Ulaan Bataar. Over the next seven decades, tons of gold were shipped out of Outer Mongolia to the USSR. These stolen Mongolian gold reserves, when added to Russia's own extensive Siberian riches, help explain how Moscow survived the Great Depression, plus how the USSR could win World War II and then go on to fight the Cold War.

*   *   *

The Chinese revolution came to a head on April 12, 1927, when Chiang Kai-shek led a *coup* in Shanghai, massacring thousands of Communists. Soviet military advisers were immediately withdrawn back to the Soviet Union. On April 18, 1927, Chiang Kai-shek then established a new Nationalist government in Nanjing, while the surviving Communists went into hiding. On August 1, 1927, Stalin ordered the Chinese Communists to stage an uprising in Nanchang. A *soviet* was established there, but it lasted only four days.

---

5 Campi, "The Political Relationship," 206.

6 Peter S.H. Tang, *Russian and Soviet Policy in Manchuria and Outer Mongolia 1911-1932* (Durham: Duke University Press, 1959), 388–389.

7 Robert Rupen, *How Mongolia is Really Ruled: A Political History of the Mongolian People's Republic 1900-1978* (Stanford, CA: Stanford University Press, 1979), 44.

Meanwhile, in Moscow, Stalin used the formation of the Nanchang *soviet* to destroy the credibility of his arch-rival Leon Trotsky. The deaths of thousands of Chinese Communists "were timed to benefit Stalin's destruction of his domestic opponents in the USSR, rather than to bring the Chinese revolution to a successful conclusion."[8] This August 1, 1927, uprising was later celebrated as the birth of the People's Liberation Army (PLA). Meanwhile, the Nationalists reunified China—on paper at least—in 1928.

After Moscow used military force to retain the Chinese Eastern Railway (CER) and Tsarist Russian territorial concessions during the 1929 Sino-Soviet War, the 1931 "Manchuria Incident" allowed Tokyo to invade Manchuria and make it a puppet state called Manchukuo. To shore up its borders with the USSR, Tokyo announced that during the next 20 years, a total of 1,000,000 Japanese households, numbering about 5,000,000 people, would move to Manchukuo. On August 2, 1937, Ambassador Uyeda and Manchukuo's Prime Minister Chang organized the Manchuria Colonization Company with 50,000,000 yuan in working capital. During its first five years, some 100,000 families—approximately 500,000 people—would be settled in Manchukuo.[9]

Moscow's response to Tokyo's mass migration of millions of Japanese to Manchukuo was predictable, especially since most of these migrants would be living in settlements along Manchukuo's lengthy northern border. Since no sane European Russian would move to Siberia willingly, the Great Purges were initiated by Stalin in September 1936 and continued through August 1938. During this short period, the number of European Russians living in Siberian labor camps, called *gulags*, quadrupled, from 500,000 in 1934 to almost 2 million in 1938.

Mass migration of people has long been used as a military strategy. But Moscow, unlike Tokyo, which could use a wide range of economic incentives to entice its citizens to move voluntarily, was simply incapable of offering comparable incentives to Russians to move to Siberia. Thus, the formation of a migration system based on labor camps—the infamous "gulag archipelago"—was arguably the only viable method available to Soviet officials for rapidly populating Siberia. While Japan eventually convinced 300,000 Japanese peasants to relocate voluntarily to Manchukuo, by the time World

---

8 Bruce A. Elleman, *Moscow and the Emergence of Communist Power in China, 1925-30: The Nanchang Uprising and the Birth of the Red Army* (London: Routledge, 2009), 207.

9 "An Outline of Manchoukuo's Second-Stage Construction Program," *Contemporary Manchuria*, Volume 1, No. 3 (September 1937), 1–15; cited in Elleman, *The Impact of Coincidence*, 35–38.

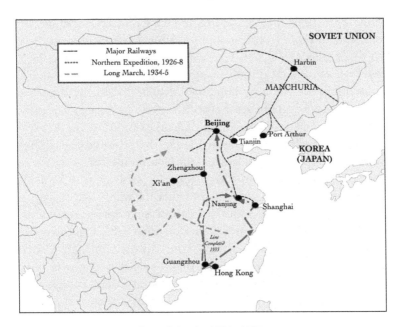

Map 3 Chinese Communist Long March, 1934–1935.

War II ended, there were almost exactly 5,000,000 Russians living in numerous gulags throughout Siberia and on the Soviet side of its border with Manchukuo. This enormous growth of Russian citizens living throughout Siberia virtually guaranteed that the Japanese could not successfully invade the USSR.

* * *

China fought Japan continuously from 1931 to 1945, even while the nationalists and Communists were fighting their own Civil War through 1949. When you add the Cold War being fought over China, there were three "nested" wars.[10] Following the "Long March" in 1934–1935, the Chinese Communists relocated to Yenan in Northwest China, close to the border with Outer Mongolia. This was one of the most isolated regions in China. For example, there were no train lines nearby to bring in troops to attack the Communists. (See Map 3.) From Yenan, they could receive Soviet aid, plus Comintern and Red Army advisers.

---

10 S.C.M. Paine, *The Wars for Asia, 1911-1949* (New York: Cambridge University Press, 2012), viii, 5.

During 1937–1945, the Nationalists and the Chinese Communists formed a second United Front to cooperate in fighting Japan. Although the USSR backed this United Front strategy, when the Soviet Red Army fought the Japanese Army to a standstill at Nomonhan near the Mongolian-Manchurian border in 1939, the resulting military stalemate led to the signing of the Soviet-Japanese Neutrality Pact of April 13, 1941. This pact guaranteed that the USSR and Japan would not attack each other for five years. As part of the secret negotiations, Moscow promised Japan that it would halt all financial and military aid to the Nationalists and the Communists in return for Tokyo's promise not to try to annihilate the Communist base areas in Yenan.[11] This pact guaranteed the CCP's survival until after the war.

China had played along with the myth of Sino-Soviet equality to exert leverage over the Western nations. In fact, what China did was play the "Soviet card." The United States trusted the Chinese diplomats. Concerned, Washington tried to match Moscow's supposedly fair treatment of China. On January 11, 1943, the United States and Great Britain completely eliminated all of their remaining extraterritorial rights and special privileges in China. But during the same year, Chiang Kai-shek for the first time confirmed "the Sino-Soviet Agreement concluded on the basis of equality was not fully carried out."[12] Unlike the West, the Soviets did not renegotiate their unequal treaties with China, instead working hand-in-hand with the Chinese Communists to consolidate the Soviet "sphere of influence" over Outer Mongolia, Manchuria, and eventually all of Mainland China.

As World War II was ending, Stalin sought to expand Communism throughout Eastern Europe. But to obtain lend-lease support from the Allies, during January 1945, Stalin promised to uphold the Yalta Conference's "Declaration on Liberated Europe," guaranteeing free elections in the Eastern European countries under his control. Stalin quickly broke his promises in Europe, and soon he would do the same in Asia too. With U.S. forces advancing toward Japan in early 1945, Stalin agreed at Yalta to abolish the five-year pact early if Russian railway concessions and ports in Manchuria were returned to Soviet control. These strategic assets would also give Moscow the ability to dominate Manchuria's sea access.

*   *   *

---

11 Bruce Elleman, "The 1940 Soviet-Japanese Secret Agreement and Its Impact on the Soviet-Iranian Supply Route," *Working Papers in International Studies*, Hoover Institution, Stanford University, January 1995.

12 Chiang Kai-shek, *China's Destiny* (New York: The MacMillan Company, 1947), 143–144; cited in Elleman, *The Impact of Coincidence*, 53–56, plus following section.

Historians have attributed Chiang Kai-shek's August 14, 1945, decision to hold a plebiscite granting Outer Mongolia full independence from China to the February 11, 1945, Yalta agreement, in which Roosevelt, Churchill, and Stalin decided: "The "status quo" in Outer-Mongolia (the Mongolian People's Republic) shall be preserved."[13] But when President Franklin Delano Roosevelt agreed to support the "status quo," he never intended to push China into granting Outer Mongolia its independence. In fact, according to international law, the juridical "status quo" was based on the May 31, 1924, Sino-Soviet Treaty, which agreed that Outer Mongolia was part of China.

But the true "status quo" was not what it appeared. China's sovereignty over Outer Mongolia was undermined by the May 31, 1924, secret protocol recognizing the existence of the 1915 tripartite treaty signed by Tsarist Russia, China, and Outer Mongolia, granting Outer Mongolia its autonomy; during 1944, the USSR even permanently annexed Tannu Tuva based on this secret diplomacy, long before Yalta was signed. Minutes of the June–August 1945 Sino-Soviet talks indicate that Stalin relied on this interpretation of "status quo." Cornered by China's 1924 secret diplomacy, Chiang agreed to Outer Mongolia's independence, but only in return for Stalin's guarantee that the USSR "give to central Chinese Government alone all moral and material support."[14] (Document 4)

It was not Yalta, therefore, but China's own secret diplomacy during the 1920s that forced Chiang Kai-shek to make a final, and ultimately futile, attempt to halt Soviet aid to the Chinese Communists. The widespread misunderstanding of what Yalta meant by "status quo" led one American scholar of Soviet history to conclude that "status quo" "implied Soviet domination of the area."[15] American scholars criticized Roosevelt for this failing: "Roosevelt did not drive a hard bargain at Yalta."[16] The secrecy surrounding the 1924 protocol also led Taiwanese historians to blame Roosevelt for giving Stalin a

---

13 Edward R. Stettinius, Jr., *Roosevelt and the Russians* (Garden City, NY: Doubleday & Company, Inc., 1949), 351.

14 "No. 1. Meeting between Marshal Stalin and Dr. Soong," 3 pages, and July 2, 1945 - August 14, 1945, "Notes taken at Sino-Soviet Conferences," 76 pages, 17, Victor Hoo Papers, Hoover Institution Archives.

15 George A. Lenson, "Yalta and the Far East," in John L. Snell, Ed., *The Meaning of Yalta* (Baton Rough: Louisiana State University Press, 1956), 157.

16 Immanuel C. Y. Hsü, *The Rise of Modern China* (New York: Oxford University Press, 1990), 608.

1) Sovereignty and administrative integrity of Manchuria. Stalin
has expressed his respect of this point for which we are very
grateful.

Stalin : Did you expect anything else from me?

Soong : I am translating textually the telegram.

For common interest of China and Russia, China is ready to afford joint
use of Port Arthur. Dairen declared an open port for period 20 years.
As to administration of Port Arthur and Dairen this should go to China
so that China has real sovereignty and administrative integrity in
Manchuria.

Molotov : Port Arthur and Dairen, both?

Soong : Yes. Chinese Eastern Railway and South Manchurian Railway main lines
to be operated jointly by Soviet Union. Profits to be divided equally.
Right of the Railways should belong to China. Branch lines, other
enterprises not connected with exploitation of railways not included
in joint administration.
Period also 20 years.

2) Sin-kiang. In the last year or so there broke out rebellion in
Sin-kiang so that communication between China and Sin-kiang broken :
trade and commerce cannot be maintained. We are anxious that Soviet
Russia, in accordance with previous agreement, co-operate with us to
eliminate trouble so that trade, communication could be resumed. Altai
range : originally belonged to Sin-kiang, should continue form part of
Sin-kiang.

3) Chinese Government. Because of Chinese communist administration
and army, who are not united within the central government, wish Soviet
Government to give to central Chinese Government alone all moral and
material support. Any assistance given to China should be confined to
the central government.

4) Outer Mongolia. Chinese government regards that since Outer
Mongolia question is the stumbling block in Sino-Soviet relations, for
common interest of Soviet Union and China and lasting peace, is ready.
after the defeat of Japan and acceptance of the three points by
Soviet Government, to grant Outer Mongolia its independence. On
this matter, in order to avoid future disputes, to go through
form of plebiscite. After plebiscite Chinese Government will
declare independence. As to area of Outer Mongolia should conform
former area set out in our maps. Chinese Government deeply hopes
Soviet Government can understand the enormous sacrifice and utmost
sincerity of the Chinese Government, so as to secure two countries
lasting and fundamental co-operation. Will you please communicate
to Stalin without any reservation."

Document 4 Chiang Kai-shek Agrees to Outer Mongolia's Independence in Return for Stalin's Support.

"powerful pretext" for encroaching on Chinese national interests, mistakenly blaming Outer Mongolia's loss on Yalta's direct reference to the "Mongolian People's Republic."[17]

---

17 Wu Hsiang-hsiang, *E-ti Ch'in-lueh Chung-kuo Shih* (A History of Imperial Russia's Invasion of China) (Taipei, Taiwan: Cheng Chung Book Company, 1954), 477; Lu Ch'iu-wen, *Chung-e Wai-meng Chiao-she Shih-mo* (The Ins and Outs of Sino-Russian

But Dr. T. V. Soong, Chiang Kai-shek's brother-in-law, as well as China's official envoy to Moscow during the 1945 Sino-Soviet negotiations, defended the American definition of "status quo": "When I left Washington I had no idea that Outer Mongolia question would be a problem. I told Truman that we might settle this question by not discussing it. I said "status quo" was that juridical sovereignty remains with China [...]. None of us had any idea Outer Mongolia would be an obstacle in our discussions." Elsewhere, Soong also explained why China hesitated to grant Outer Mongolia its independence: "If we are to recognize "status quo" in Mongolia which has many times been recognized by Soviet Union as integral part of China our position as a government will be badly shaken before our people."[18]

The diplomatic pressure that Stalin could exert on China came not from the Yalta agreement but from the 1924 secret protocol. This helps to explain why Chiang Kai-shek was willing to use Outer Mongolian independence as a bargaining chip in his secret negotiations with Stalin. On July 9, 1945, Chiang Kai-shek sent a telegram stating, "Chinese government now willing make greatest sacrifice in the utmost sincerity to find fundamental solution of Chinese/Soviet relations" by agreeing to grant Outer Mongolia its independence in return for Soviet guarantees to uphold China's territorial integrity in Xinjiang and Manchuria, in addition to the following condition: "Because of Chinese communist administration and army, who are not united within the central government, wish Soviet Government to give to central Chinese Government alone all moral and material support. Any assistance given to China should be confined to the central government."[19]

Thereafter, in the Sino-Soviet Treaty of Friendship and Alliance signed on August 14, 1945, Vyacheslav Molotov included the following note: "In accordance with the spirit of the aforementioned treaty, and in order to put into effect its aims and purposes, the Government of the USSR agrees to render to China moral support and aid in military supplies and other material resources, such support and aid to be entirely given to the National Government as the Central Government of China."[20]

Negotiations on Outer Mongolia) (Taipei, Taiwan: Cheng-wen Publishing Company, 1976), 242–247.

18 July 2, 1945 - August 14, 1945, "Notes taken at Sino-Soviet Conferences," 13–16.

19 Ibid.

20 January 31, 1952, "Statement by United States Delegate John Sherman Cooper in the Political Committee of the United Nations General Assembly in the Discussion of Threats to the Political Independence and Territorial Integrity of China, at Paris, France, January 28, 1952." Hoover Institution Archives, Maxwell Hamilton collection, Box #1.

These conditions prove that Chiang agreed to recognize Outer Mongolia's independence only in exchange for Stalin's promise not to support the Communists in the ongoing Civil War. Outer Mongolia has always been portrayed by the USSR and China as a separate independent country, but this subterfuge was adopted to protect China's national honor, in other words, a way to save China from "losing face." To preserve China's dignity, it was Chiang Kai-shek who suggested holding a fake plebiscite in Outer Mongolia. This plebiscite was merely for form's sake, however, which helps to explain why China did not dispute the results when it was later reported that 98.14 percent of Outer Mongolia's electorate, many of them nomadic herdsmen, voted in the hastily-arranged plebiscite, all of them for independence from China.[21] The Nationalist government thereafter officially recognized Outer Mongolia's complete independence from China on January 1, 1946.

* * *

By early August 1945, only a detailed agreement as to where exactly the Sino-Soviet boundary ran was left unresolved. With Japan's surrender imminent, it was important to Chiang Kai-shek that the agreement on Outer Mongolia be announced soon, so that the Chinese people could be convinced that Outer Mongolia's loss was a necessity of war. On July 11, 1945, Soong expressed his concern that the joint Sino-Soviet declaration on Outer Mongolia not mention the border, since there were still many disagreements about the boundary line. Stalin agreed, suggesting that they retain the "status quo," but Soong retorted: "These is dispute about "status quo"."[22]

Negotiations were broken off after July 12, so that Stalin and Molotov could attend the conference at Potsdam, but talks resumed once again on August 7. On August 10, Stalin disputed the maps that Soong had brought back with him: "Re frontiers Chinese map is not well founded. Existing frontiers should be recognized."[23] Stalin stuck to his proposal because the existing borders actually included extensive Manchurian territories that the Japanese government had secretly ceded to Moscow during Outer Mongolia-Manchukuo border negotiations in the 1930s.

The Chinese delegation, on the other hand, pleaded with Stalin to define the border between Outer Mongolia and China, even suggesting that the two

---

21 Max Beloff, *Soviet Far Eastern Policy Since Yalta* (New York: Institute of Pacific Relations, 1950), 9; cited in Elleman, *The Impact of Coincidence*, 57–59, plus following section.
22 July 2, 1945 - August 14, 1945, "Notes taken at Sino-Soviet Conferences," 31.
23 Ibid., 47–49.

countries use a Chinese college atlas as their guide. But Stalin advocated that the current borders be respected:

> Frontiers existing for 26 years was established without any disputes with China. Our topographers went there and drew on map a line which separated Chinese and Mongolian guards. That's west and south. Re east there were disputes with Japanese. Then there was an agreement concluded. If we re-examine, it will take time, certain pieces will be taken, others given. Your Russian map is not valid.

After an intense debate, the Chinese delegation insisted that all they wanted was "clarity" and that "we want to know where the line is." But Stalin was determined not to discuss the border, pointing out that China had never challenged the border before, to which Soong replied: "We always considered Outer Mongolia as Chinese and there was no need to challenge."[24]

Stalin was aided by the strict time limit, since once Japan surrendered, it would become more difficult to convince the Chinese people that the Nationalists' concessions were necessary. On August 13, 1945, Soong backed down and resolved the borders in a haphazard fashion: "Chiang wanted agree[ment] on boundaries first, but Stalin said it would take too much time. So Chiang accepts existing boundaries. That question is therefore excluded from questions to be settled." With Soong's concession, not only did Stalin gain China's official recognition of the USSR's long-standing hold over Outer Mongolia, but the expanded borders, which the Soviets had formerly negotiated with Japan during the 1930s, remained unchanged, all in return for what would soon prove to be Stalin's empty promise to support only Chiang Kai-shek and the Nationalists.[25]

* * *

At Yalta, Stalin had also convinced Roosevelt and Churchill to grant the USSR a "preeminent" position in Manchuria, emphasizing Soviet control over the CER that traversed the region to the naval base at Port Arthur. The term "preeminent" was widely understood to mean "in regard to other powers, not to China." During Sino-Soviet talks held in July–August 1945, however, Stalin claimed that this also meant greater power than China. For example, Port Arthur would become a Soviet concession area for 30 years,

---

24 Ibid., 53–54.
25 Ibid., 70.

and in times of war the Soviet government would administer the nearby civilian port of Dalian.[26]

After entering the war against Japan during August 1945, Stalin quickly consolidated his gains in Manchuria, militarizing Port Arthur and the nearby civilian port at Dalian. Beginning in August 1945, the Soviet Navy helped move Communists into Manchuria by sea. With Soviet assistance, tens of thousands of Communist troops entered southern Manchuria from the Shandong Peninsula, where Communist forces were reportedly also being supplied by Soviet ships from Dalian.[27] Once in Manchuria, the PLA used the Soviet-controlled railways to move quickly into the major cities. From Manchuria, the Chinese Communists then spread throughout all of Mainland China.

A secret protocol in the August 14, 1945, Sino-Soviet Friendship Treaty gave the USSR full control over offshore islands, allowing it to blockade access to Port Arthur and Dalian. (Map 4) This put the USSR in a position to dominate most of Manchuria's littoral, including sea denial throughout the Bo Hai Gulf and the Yellow Sea. As early as November 1945, Chinese Nationalist officials complained to British foreign secretary Ernest Bevin that Soviet sea control over Manchuria's ports meant the Nationalists could not carry out a total occupation of Manchuria.[28] By November 1948, the Nationalist government stated that "the most fundamental factor in the general deterioration of the military situation [in Manchuria] was the nonobservance by the Soviet Union of the [August 1945] Sino-Soviet Treaty of Friendship and Alliance."[29]

*   *   *

As World War II was ending, Stalin defended the USSR's imperialist actions in China, citing Outer Mongolia's strategic importance. But the aggressive nature of Moscow's foreign policy was made especially clear after the success of the Chinese Communist revolution in 1949, when Moscow refused to open negotiations with the PRC on the status of Outer Mongolia and continued to occupy it until the collapse of the USSR in 1991. In the

---

26 Elleman, *Diplomacy and Deception*, 231–251.

27 "Dairen Port Closed to Foreign Ships," *North China Daily News*, August 21, 1947, FO 371/6335, TNA/UK.

28 Report of Discussion between Ernest Bevin and Chinese Ambassador, November 20, 1945, FO 371/46271, TNA/UK.

29 Steven I. Levine, *Anvil of Victory: The Communist Revolution in Manchuria, 1945-1948* (New York: Columbia University Press, 1987), 287.

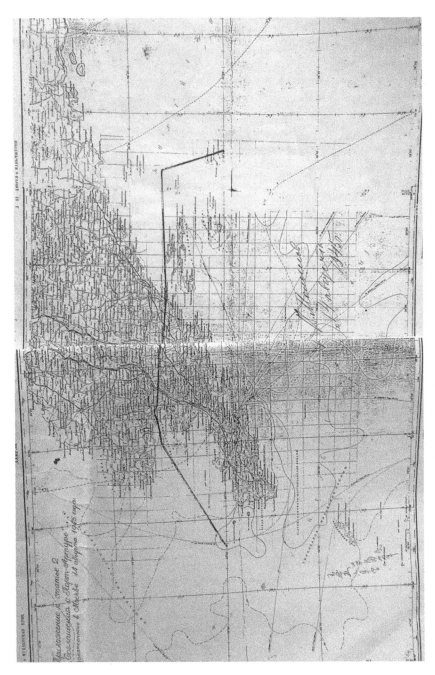

Map 4 Secret Protocol to the 1945 Sino-Soviet Friendship Treaty.

meantime, billions of dollars of natural resources, including, most importantly, gold, continued to be removed from Outer Mongolia.

Stalin's control over Outer Mongolia, plus much of Manchuria through 1955 helped the Chinese Communists take power throughout Mainland China. But after the PRC was formed on October 1, 1949, Outer Mongolia's status as a Soviet protectorate continued over the protests of the Chinese Communists like Mao Zedong, who felt it had been promised to him. Soviet leaders also adamantly refused to reopen border negotiations with China, a dispute that continued to plague Sino-Soviet relations during the following decades.[30] By resorting to secret diplomacy, Soviet diplomats acquired an estimated 600,000 square miles of territory from China. This diplomatic victory rivaled the heyday of Tsarist Russia's nineteenth-century territorial expansion, when China ceded approximately 665,000 square miles of territory to Russia.[31] Without Outer Mongolia, the amount of territory secured by Russia was approximately five times the area of Japan and more than seven times that of the United Kingdom; including Outer Mongolia, this territory exceeded all of India and was more than one-third the size of the United States.

Sino-Soviet negotiating records confirm that Soviet diplomats resorted to secret diplomacy to complete the Tsarist Russian goal of separating Outer Mongolia from China and adding it to the Soviet bloc. These diplomatic records prove that Russia's foreign policy remained constant from the 1850s to 1945. Soviet expansionism was simply the most recent stage of Tsarist Russian imperialism, with China as its latest victim. While Moscow actively intervened in the Civil War against Chiang Kai-shek and on the side of Mao Zedong and the Communists, Sino-Soviet tensions were destined to increase after 1949 over the status of Outer Mongolia, Manchuria, and the precise location of the Sino-Soviet border.

---

30 August 1, 1964, "An Interview with Chou En-lai," in Dennis J. Doolin, Ed., *Territorial Claims in the Sino-Soviet Conflict* (Stanford, CA: Hoover Institution Studies: 7, 1965), 45.

31 Alan J. Day, Ed., *Border and Territorial Disputes*, Keesings Reference Publication (Detroit: Gale Research Co., 1982), 259–261.

Chapter C

THE CHINA CONUNDRUM

The greatest prize in the Cold War was China. Europe was important too, of course, but immediately after World War II, it was divided into East and West, and this division remained basically unchanged for the next 50 years. Many assumed that after World War II, the U.S. government made a mistake by not fighting in China against the Communists, but the U.S. government's main strategic goal was to try to break up the Sino-Soviet alliance. To make this happen, it was better for the Chinese Communists to dominate all of Mainland China. Only then could Sino-Soviet tensions rise and be sufficiently brittle to break apart the Soviet bloc.

*　*　*

Sino-Soviet tensions were already poor even before Mao Zedong proclaimed victory on October 1, 1949. In August 1948, British officials reported that Russians in the port of Dalian in Manchuria had begun to exclude not just Nationalist forces but also "the armed forces of the Chinese Communists."[1] Soon after this British report, the Central Intelligence Agency (CIA) in December 1948 recommended that the Chinese Communists be allowed to dominate all of Mainland China without American opposition, since there would probably be "no chance of a split within the Party or between the Party and the USSR," until after the "Communist domination of China."[2] (Document 5) As Nationalist rule imploded in China in the late 1940s, President Harry S. Truman decided it was not worth billions of dollars and millions of men to defend Chiang Kai-shek's corrupt government. U.S. military advisers were "unanimous in the view that short of the actual

---

1 Letter from British Embassy in Nanking to Foreign Office, August 13, 1948, WO 208/4571, TNA/UK; cited in Elleman, *The Impact of Coincidence*, 61–64, plus following section.
2 Central Intelligence Agency (CIA), Chinese Communist Capabilities for Control of all China, Secret, December 10, 1948, Harry S. Truman Presidential Library (HSTPL).

...ing them increased popular support. ...The Communist... ...
economic situation in North and Central China to the point where any Communist
program appears more desirable to the people than a Nationalist survival.
        A Communist-dominated government will probably come to power as a result of
what is in effect the surrender of the National Government. This government will probably be proclaimed as a "coalition," and it will include many non-Communists, among
them members of the present National Government. As a "coalition" it will have the
advantage of not necessarily forfeiting international recognition. It is almost certain,
however, that Communist officials will dictate the policies of such a government.
        There is no doubt that the Chinese Communist Party has been and is an instru-
ment of Soviet policy. While there is no guarantee that the USSR will always find the
Chinese Communists dependable, there appears to be no chance of a split within the
Party or between the Party and the USSR until the time of Communist domination
of China.

Note: The information in this report is as of 1 December 1948.
      The intelligence organizations of the Departments of State, Army, Navy, and the Air Force
      have concurred in this report.

Document 5 Central Intelligence Agency's December 1948 Recommendation that
the Chinese Communists be Allowed to Dominate all of Mainland China.

employment of US troops in China no amount of military assistance can now
save the Chiang Kai-shek regime in the face of the present political, military
and economic deterioration."[3]

Once the Communists took all of Mainland China, it was imperative
to make Mao Zedong as dependent on Russia as possible, so as to increase
Sino-Soviet tensions. Prior to Mao's visit to Moscow in early 1950, therefore, Washington refused to recognize Beijing, which meant "the Chinese
Communists cannot now play off one great power against another, since
they have no non-Soviet allies at the moment."[4] As early as January 2, 1950,
Truman was told that China would never follow the "Moscow line" because
the "Chinese are not built that way." In addition, due to the potency of
the "Asia for the Asiatics" movement, the Russians were "not accepted by
Orientals as Asiatics."[5]

Truman's goal was instead to push the USSR and China closer together,
with the ultimate goal of breaking them apart. After the Korean War began
in June 1950, the U.S. government adopted a "sea denial" strategy by sending the Seventh Fleet into the Taiwan Strait to stop a planned PRC invasion

---

3 Summary of Telegrams, TOP SECRET, November 8, 1948, PHST, SMOF-Naval
  Aide, Box 23, State Department Briefs File, HSTPL.
4 Summary of Telegrams, Top Secret, November 27, 1949, HSTPL.
5 Letter from H. T. Goodier to Harry S. Truman, January 2, 1950, PHST, Official File,
  OF 150-G, Box 761, Formosa, HSTPL; underlining in the original.

of Taiwan, in the process creating the Taiwan Patrol Force. Typically, four U.S. Navy ships were sent to Taiwan at a time, with two of them cruising up and down the Taiwan Strait in opposite directions, acting as a "tripwire" in case of a PRC attack. Assuming a U.S. Navy ship was shot at or sunk, then the entire Seventh Fleet could be called in to assist. This buffer patrol lasted for 29 years until January 1, 1979, the longest such naval operation in modern history.[6]

On December 23, 1950, Washington put extreme economic pressure on China by adopting a strategic embargo. Called the Coordinating Committee for Multilateral Export Controls (COCOM), the various strategic categories were divided into I, II, and III subdivisions. This embargo lasted for 21 years, through June 10, 1971, also one of the longest in modern history. In fall 1952, after Japan joined COCOM, the China Committee (CHINCOM) instituted even tighter strategic controls on China, including banning industrial machinery, steel mill products, and metal of all types. Greece and Turkey joined in 1953, and Sweden and Switzerland agreed to cooperate, meaning all NATO countries (minus Iceland), plus Japan and the United States, were now members.

In August 1954, when COCOM relaxed some of its export controls on Russia and Eastern Europe, there was no equivalent relaxation for China. This difference between exports to the USSR and the PRC became known as the "China Differential."[7] This differential continued at varying levels of intensity for the rest of the Cold War. Due to tighter sanctions on China, Secretary of State John Foster Dulles stated that all participating countries "instituted and maintained controls on strategic trade with Communist China that are much more severe and sweeping than the system applicable to Soviet Russia and the rest of the Soviet bloc."[8]

* * *

The China differential helped exacerbate Sino-Soviet tensions, especially when combined with a Nationalist-enforced naval blockade of southeastern

---

6 Bruce A. Elleman, *High Sea's Buffer: The Taiwan Patrol Force, 1950-1979* (Newport, RI: NWC Press, 2012).

7 Motoyuki Takamatsu, "The Eisenhower Administration's Response to the China Differential, 1955-57," *International Relations*, No. 105 (January 1994), 9–10 (English abstract), 60–79.

8 Letter from John Foster Dulles to J. Bracken Lee, Governor of Utah, December 30, 1953, D-H-2, Dulles Dec (53), Dwight David Eisenhower Presidential Library (DDEPL).

China from 1949–1958. The naval blockade stopped a large percentage of foreign goods from being delivered to China. Beijing had no choice but to trade primarily with the USSR and various Eastern European countries by means of the Trans-Siberian Railway. Due to the COCOM strategic embargo and especially the CHINCOM rules that made the embargo against China even stricter, Beijing had to pay much higher rates to import these strategic goods.

Sino-Soviet diplomatic tensions grew gradually worse over time. According to a 1952 agreement, all Soviet military forces were supposed to withdraw from the Manchurian ports by May 31, 1955. Moscow also agreed to transfer "the installations in the area of the Port Arthur [Lüshun] naval base to the Government of the People's Republic of China." But at the last minute, the first secretary of the Communist Party of the USSR, Nikita Khrushchev, refused to transfer the artillery protecting this base from attack by sea. Instead, Khrushchev demanded that China must pay the full price for these guns: "These are very expensive weapons, we would be selling them at reduced prices."[9]

Moscow's decision during spring 1955 to strip the Port Arthur naval base of its main defensive weapons left China highly vulnerable in Manchuria. Khrushchev's decision not to give these advanced weapons to Mao appeared intentional. During May 1955, Dulles had secretly told Molotov during meetings in Vienna that "we had obtained from the Chinese Nationalists arrangements which we thought would enable us to influence the situation for peace from our side and he suggested that the Soviet Union could do the same with the Chinese Communists," in particular since "the Chinese Communists were dependent upon Russia for various strategic supplies and planes and could not develop their plans without Russian support."[10]

Khrushchev's decision to strip the port defenses from Manchuria was a clear sign that the USSR was unwilling to back Mao's offensive to retake various offshore islands from Taiwan. He further hinted that the USSR's nuclear umbrella might not cover the Taiwan Strait. Meanwhile, fear of Communist expansion along the first island chain led the U.S. government to increase its support to Taiwan during the two Taiwan Strait crises in 1954–1955 and 1958. Washington also felt pressured to sign security treaties supporting Chiang Kai-shek's efforts to defend a number of offshore islands from PRC attacks.

---

9 Nikita Sergeevich Khrushchev and Sergei Khrushchev, *Memoirs of Nikita Khrushchev: Statesman, 1953-1964* (College Park: Penn State Press, 2007), 434.

10 Conversation at Ambassador's Residence, Vienna on May 14, 1955, TOP SECRET, May 17, 1955, DDE Subject Series Box 70, State, Dept. of (May 1955), 2, DDEPL.

During 1958, when Khrushchev tried to convince Mao of the value of retaining the floundering Sino-Soviet naval coalition, Khrushchev reminded Mao: "On the issue of Port Arthur [...] it was advantageous for you that the Soviet Army was in Port Arthur and Manchuria."[11] But the USSR's exclusionist tactics in Manchuria, which were extremely successful during the late 1940s against the Nationalists, proved to be a double-edged sword, undermining the foundations of the Sino-Soviet alliance. By the late 1950s, Washington's strategy was so successful that it resulted in a Sino-Soviet split.

Washington's use of military and economic pressure to create the Sino-Soviet split was a strategic victory. Combining the Nationalist naval blockade with a strategic embargo that included a China differential proved to be a powerful weapon. Meanwhile, Sino-Soviet tensions were further exacerbated by the presence of the Seventh Fleet's Taiwan Patrol Force, which stopped the PRC from attacking Taiwan. Truman's decision to let Mao Zedong and the Communists take all of Mainland China proved to be a huge strategic success. Over time, rising tensions resulted in the Sino-Soviet split during 1959, just as the CIA had predicted would happen a decade earlier, in December 1948.

*   *   *

Under President Lyndon Baines Johnson, the Vietnam War was used as a peripheral campaign to exacerbate Sino-Soviet tensions even further, this time to turn them into actual enemies. In January 1965, McGeorge Bundy warned Johnson that he and Bob McNamara believed that "our current policy [in Vietnam] can lead only to disastrous defeat," but Washington could "use our military power in the Far East [...] to force a change in Communist policy."[12] Soviet arms deliveries to North Vietnam via China were the weak link, especially SAMs (Surface-to-Air Missile). A Top Secret CIA report from February 22, 1965, stated "that Kosygin's trip to Hanoi will result in the Soviets giving 'defensive' aid to North Vietnam in the form of fighter planes, SAMs and radar equipment."[13]

---

11 *Cold War International History Project Bulletin*, Issue 12/13 (Fall/Winter 2001), 254–255.

12 McGeorge Bundy, "Memorandum for the President," Secret, January 27, 1965, National Security Council History, Deployment of Major U.S. Forces to Vietnam, July 1965, Vol. 1, Lyndon Baines Johnson Presidential Library (LBJPL).

13 CIA Memorandum, "The Situation in Vietnam," Top Secret Dinar/Declassified with Redactions 7/22/1999, February 22, 1965, Box 49, Folder 3, Document 28a, National Security File, Country File, Vietnam, LBJPL; cited in Elleman, *The Impact of Coincidence*, 71–74; plus this section.

Beginning in 1965, Moscow felt obliged to provide North Vietnam with SAMs. On March 28, 1965, the CIA reported the USSR, China, and North Vietnam had signed an agreement to transport arms shipments across China by railway. Sea transport was impossible: "Moscow has shown itself reluctant to date to ship extensive aid to North Vietnam by sea, and recent Soviet allusions to an 'American blockade' suggest that the USSR fears a repetition of Khrushchev's disastrous backdown in the face of the US naval quarantine in the Cuban Missile Crisis." But Beijing had already placed strict limits on the transit of Soviet personnel. Presidium member Mikhail Suslov complained that "although the Chinese had agreed to let Soviet nationals go through China by rail, they had 'changed their minds several times in this regard'."[14] On April 27, 1965, the CIA predicted that the post-Khrushchev leadership "feels compelled to act, even in the face of risks which Khrushchev had turned away from."[15]

Transporting missiles to Hanoi by train required Beijing's active cooperation. A May 1967 report by Walt Rostow pointed out that due to Vietnam's geographical location, "Moscow cannot feasibly undertake any serious military participation in the war, with its own combat forces, far from the sources of Soviet power, and at the end of lines of communication passing through the dubiously friendly territory of China or risking US counteraction at sea."[16] But funneling the SAMs through China meant that Moscow's "special area of responsibility" to provide Hanoi with a viable air defense was its most vulnerable Achilles Heel.[17]

According to Gordan Chang, President Dwight D. Eisenhower's top priority was to break apart the Sino-Soviet monolith, so in his 1963 memoir *The White House Years*, he barely mentioned Sino-Soviet relations, so as "to avoid saying anything that could hinder the emergence of the Sino-Soviet split."[18] Johnson's strategy to interfere with the delivery of SAMs was specifically designed to attack this critical Center of Gravity in the Sino-Soviet

---

14 CIA Memorandum, "Status of Soviet Military Assistance to North Vietnam," Top Secret/Declassified with Redactions 11/24/1981, March 15, 1965, Box 49, Folder 4, Document 5, National Security File, Country File, Vietnam, LBJPL.

15 CIA Memorandum, "Future Soviet Moves in Vietnam," April 27, 1965, Box 16, Folder 3, Document 99, National Security File, Country File, Vietnam, LBJPL.

16 Walt Rostow to the President, Memorandum, Secret/Declassified 8/14/1995, May 5, 1967, NSF Country File Vietnam, Box 43, Folder 1, Document 47, LBJPL.

17 CIA, National Intelligence Estimate Number 11-16-66, "Current Soviet Attitudes Toward the US," Secret/Sanitized 6/23/2008, July 28, 1966, NSF National Intelligence Estimates, Box 3, Folder 6, Document 23, LBJPL.

18 Gordan H. Chang, *Friends and Enemies: The United States, China, and the Soviet Union, 1948-1972* (Stanford, CA: Stanford University Press, 1990), 331, n24.

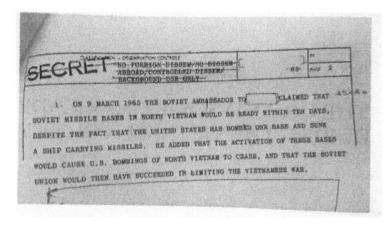

Document 6 A Soviet ambassador Acknowledged on 9 March 1965 that a Soviet Ship Carrying Missiles had been Sunk.

relationship. In a nutshell, Moscow was trapped by its landlocked geography and by its open-ended commitments to Hanoi.

* * *

On March 9, 1965, a Soviet ambassador acknowledged the United States had bombed one Surface-to-Air Missile (SAM) base in Vietnam, plus sank "a ship carrying missiles."[19] (Document 6) Frustrated by the secret American naval blockade that forced the USSR to use only land routes through China during March 1965, one Soviet official even admitted that Washington's policy "is coming dangerously close to 'boxing in' the governing authorities in the USSR," and he warned that "Communist China would be the only winner in the event of a miscalculation by either the US or the Soviet Union."[20] (Document 7)

According to one Russian-language source from 2009, Moscow shipped 7,658 SAMs to Hanoi during the Vietnam War.[21] Each one cost about $100,000 and, with its launcher, took an entire train car to transport. Thus,

---

19 CIA Memorandum, "Alleged Imminent Stationing of Soviet Missiles," Secret/Sanitized, March 15, 1965, Box 15, Folder 2, Document 118, National Security File, Country File, Vietnam, LBJPL.

20 CIA Memorandum, "The Situation in Vietnam," Top Secret/Sanitized, March 20, 1965, Box 49, Folder 5, Document 17, National Security File, Country File, Vietnam, LBJPL.

21 Alexander Okorokov, *CCCP v Borbe za Mirovoe Gospodstvo* (Moscow: Eksmo, 2009), 134.

> 15. The remarks of a Soviet UN official, in a
> recent conversation with a US national, emphasized
> the policy dilemma which confronts Moscow as a result
> of US air actions against North Vietnam.
>
> 16. The official, ... asserted that the method
> and intensity of US escalation is coming dangerously
> close to "boxing in" the governing authorities in the
> USSR. He repeated the line taken by other Soviet of-
> ficials in private conversation with Western officials
> that Communist China would be the only winner in the
> event of a miscalculation by either the US or the So-
> viet Union.

Document 7 During March 1965 a Soviet Official Admitted that Washington's Policy was 'Boxing in' the USSR.

every SAM transferred through China added incrementally to Sino-Soviet frictions. In 1965, Moscow sent Hanoi 80 million dollars' worth of SAMs and launchers, or about 60 percent of the $142,000,000 million in Soviet military aid.[22] By February 16, 1966, it was reported that North Vietnam now had 84 SAM sites, which was an increase of 21 sites during recent weeks.[23]

Washington's secret goal was to force the Soviets to ship even more SAMs through China. While only 200 SAMs were provided in 1965 and 1,100 in 1966, in just the first six months of 1967 alone, an estimated 1,750 SAMs were shipped to North Vietnam through China, one of the largest components of the $220 million in Soviet aid.[24] Washington's strategic goal was to add pressure to this critical supply line. As Rostow told Johnson on February 11, 1967, "the trouble in China may affect supplies to Hanoi," which makes it "clear the Chinese are trying to force a break in relations with Moscow."[25]

* * *

American bomber runs sought to soak up the maximum number of SAMs, since importing new ones through China directly exacerbated Sino-Soviet

22 CIA statistics, Top Secret Trine, June 1, 1966, NSF Country File Vietnam, Box 51, Folder 4, Document 49b, LBJPL.

23 CIA, "Intelligence Memorandum, DRV SAM Defense Expanding," Top Secret, February 16, 1966, NSF Country File Vietnam, Box 51, Folder 2, Document 25, LBJPL.

24 CIA, "Intelligence Memorandum: Assessment of a Postulated Agreement on US and Soviet Actions in North Vietnam," Top Secret Trine, August 4, 1967, NSF Country File Vietnam, Box 51, Folder 5, Document 27, LBJPL.

25 Letter from W.W.R. to the President, Top Secret, February 11, 1967, NSF Country File Vietnam, Box 51, Folder 3, Document 10, LBJPL.

tensions. The SAMs posed a huge threat to American planes. But as of August 17, 1966, only 26 planes had been shot down by SAMs, as compared to 272 brought down by AA fire: "Surface-to-Air missile defenses have played a significant role in inflicting losses, not by direct effects, but by forcing attack aircraft down into the range of anti-aircraft guns." Still, the 384 lost aircraft out of 100,784 sorties equaled only 0.3 percent, "which has been somewhat less than predicted."[26]

Of course, U.S. pilots were never told that the real goal behind bombing North Vietnam was to soak up as many SAMs as possible. Chief of Naval Operations David McDonald reported that aircrews criticized repetitive air attacks that seemed more than anything else to benefit enemy gunners. When Senator Symington visited South Vietnam during late 1966, he made a point of emphasizing to Westmoreland that "restrictions relative to attack on targets in North Vietnam impact unfavorably on US pilot morale," and he opposed "repetitive pilot tours."[27]

These criticisms actually confirmed that the true goal of the bombing was to soak up the maximum number of SAMs as possible. During the *Rolling Thunder* operation, 108 aircraft out of 14,557 sorties were shot down, and by the second year, 362 U.S. aircraft had been lost. In late November 1967, the White House situation room reported that because the bombing was focused on Hanoi, which had the best air defenses, "new records were set in the number of US aircraft downed (18), in the number of surface-to-air missiles fired in one week (299) and in the number of US aircraft downed by missiles in one week (10)."[28] Many pilots were rescued, but many others became POWs. For example, John McCain's A4 was shot down by a SAM while attacking the Hanoi Thermal Power Plant on October 26, 1967, and he spent several years as a POW.

*   *   *

---

26 Memorandum by Arthur McCaffety for the President entitled "U.S. Bombing Missions over North Vietnam," Secret/Declassified on 3/18/1994, August 17, 1966, NSF Country File-Vietnam, Box 35, Folder 2, Document 108, LBJPL.

27 Memorandum, "To the President from General Westmoreland in Saigon," Secret/ Declassified 1/30/1984, January 3, 1967, Box 39, Folder 3, Document 115a, National Security File, Country File, Vietnam, LBJPL.

28 White House Situation Room to the President, "Situation Room Report for the President," Top Secret/Declassified 6/3/1993, November 25, 1967, NSF Country File Vietnam, Box 104, Folder 2, Document 76, LBJPL.

Bombing operations against Hanoi exerted incredible political pressure on Moscow and Beijing. On June 2, 1966, this operation's impact was boiled down, and it was determined that the bombing "has increased, not diminished, tensions among Communist states—especially between Chinese and Soviets." News of the success of the anti-SAM campaign was included in the original "secret" version of an Alternatives Paper written by Bill Jorden. As Rostow told Johnson on June 2, 1966, this section was removed from the "boiled down and sanitized version of the Alternatives Paper," probably because it was considered to be the single most important—so also the most highly sensitive if inadvertently leaked—part of the report.[29] By June 1968, only one American plane was shot down by a SAM the entire month, perhaps due to the strain put on the Communist Bloc's logistical system.

In early 1967, Edwin Reischauer warned that air strikes represented "a complete psychological blunder" in believing that "the bombing can punish the enemy enough to make him want to negotiate."[30] But this was never the main reason for bombing North Vietnam. During December 1966, the CIA reported Hanoi thought "the Vietnam war was a test case as to whether world communism would succeed or not."[31] The most important strategic goal of the anti-SAM campaign, therefore, was to ramp up pressure, break apart the Sino-Soviet alliance, and then undermine Communism and win the Cold War.

Soaking up SAMs was critical to this plan's success. By February 1967, the CIA could report: "The internal turmoil in China with its anti-Soviet theme has greatly reduced the amount of Soviet aid reaching North Vietnam. The Soviets have tried to bypass the problem by transporting the material by air but lack sufficient long-range planes to accomplish the task."[32] On March 23, 1967, the CIA reported Moscow was trying to fly military materiel destined for North Vietnam via India, Burma, and Laos to avoid complications by the

---

29 Sanitized Version of the Alternatives Paper by Bill Jorden, Walt Rostow Papers, June 2, 1966, NSF Country File Vietnam, Box 33, Folder 5, Document 2456, LBJPL.

30 Memorandum entitled "Edwin Reischauer on Vietnam," 1-2 February 1967, Box 40, Folder 5, Document 131, National Security File, Country File, Vietnam, LBJPL.

31 CIA Intelligence Information Cable, "Comments on the Vietnam Situation and Relations with Various Foreign Countries," Secret/Declassified and Sanitized 6/11/1998, December 19, 1966, Box 40, Folder 158, Document 105a, National Security File, Country File, Vietnam, LBJPL.

32 CIA Intelligence Information Cable, "State of Morale in North Vietnam and Sincerity of Willingness to Negotiate Peace," Secret/Declassified and Sanitized 4/15/1993, February 7, 1967, Box 40, Folder 4, Document 105a, National Security File, Country File, Vietnam, LBJPL.

Chinese Communists.[33] During July 1968, Beijing for the first time absolutely refused to allow "three trains of materiel destined for Vietnam [to] transit Chinese territory."[34] This undermined their Vietnam cooperation and deepened hostile feelings between Moscow and Beijing.

* * *

Shipping delays, especially for SAMs, negatively impacted Sino-Soviet relations. Once it became clear that a Sino-Soviet war was imminent, Johnson ordered all air, naval, and artillery bombardment of North Vietnam to end on November 1, 1968. His stated goal was to open talks leading to a negotiated peace settlement, but arguably another important goal was to let tensions fester between Beijing and Moscow. Johnson's plan succeeded. The Chinese decision to stop the munitions trains proved that Johnson's peripheral campaign in Vietnam had been an enormous success.

On March 2, 1969, fighting erupted along China's northern border with the USSR. For a time, it even appeared that this conflict might expand and perhaps even turn into a nuclear war. The Soviet government immediately condemned the fighting and blamed it on China, calling them "intentional actions planned in advance." As a March 29, 1969, Soviet statement explained, only after much effort, Soviet frontier guards "drove the violators from Soviet territory." Moscow appeared to understand exactly what Washington was planning to do in the near future, since the official Soviet statement then said: "Such events can only be good news to those who in all and any way would like to create an abyss of enmity between the Soviet Union and the People's Republic of China."[35] According to a State Department memo from March 18, 1969, the Chinese had bitten off more than they could chew, and once the Soviets called their bluff, they had no choice but to "dig in" if they did not want to risk losing face by retreating.

The 1969 Sino-Soviet war along China's northern border led to a complete rupture between Moscow and Beijing. Later, the Acting Foreign Minister of China told Kissinger during his October 1971 secret visit that: "What the PRC wanted was (a) an acceptance by the USSR that the treaties had in

---

33 CIA Intelligence Information Cable entitled "Comments of North Vietnamese Diplomat," Secret/Declassified and Sanitized on 4/27/1993, March 23, 1967, NSF Country File-Vietnam, Box 35, Folder 3, Document 153, LBJPL.

34 Telegram from American Embassy Paris to SecState Washington, July 24, 1968, Secret/Declassified 11/5/2013. NSF Country File-France, Box 173, LBJPL.

35 "USSR Government Statement," March 29, 1969, Box 709, File 3, Richard M. Nixon Presidential Library (RMNPL).

fact been unequal, and (b) a delineation of the border in minor aspects such as putting the demarcation line into the middle of rivers instead of on the Chinese side as the Soviets claim. Also, he said, the Soviets had pushed troops into all disputed territories [...] this was unacceptable."[36]

This Sino-Soviet border dispute gave President Richard M. Nixon a chance to combine forces with China to exert greater pressure on the USSR and, over the long term, induce its economic and military collapse. Coincidentally, now that soaking up the maximum number of SAMs was no longer necessary, on March 3, 1969, the U.S. Navy Top Gun School opened. One of this school's goals was to train U.S. pilots on how to better avoid being hit by SAMs.

* * *

By now, the Sino-Soviet split was complete. Knowing full well that Moscow feared a two-front war against both East and West, a Top Secret memo from June 1969 concluded that the Russian government needed "a continued deployment of major U.S. military forces in Asia," "some form of acquiescence or at least non-opposition to their plan for a regional security arrangement against the Chinese," and "they need us to lean to the Moscow side of the Sino-Soviet dispute and not start our own maneuvering directed to Peking." This memo then concluded that if Russia did not cooperate in ending the Vietnam War, it would "force us to deal directly with Peking."[37]

On June 24, 1969, Al Haig sent a Top Secret memo to Kissinger discussing how worried the USSR was that the United States "should, if we have not already started to, exploit the differences between the Soviet Union and Communist China."[38] On August 4, 1969, Nixon called Moscow the main aggressor in the Sino-Soviet war and argued that a Chinese defeat would be contrary to U.S. government interests. Nixon sought to open diplomatic talks with Beijing by engaging in confidential "signaling." The student demonstration at Kent State University on May 4, 1970, was perhaps a Chinese "signal" back to Nixon, since the 51st anniversary of the May 4, 1919 movement held great meaning for Chinese revolutionaries. In the immediate aftermath

---

36 Memorandum of Conversation between Prime Minister Chou En-lai and Assistant to the President for National Security Affairs Henry A. Kissinger, October 21, 1971, Top Secret/Declassified, Box 846, File 1, RMNPL.

37 Memorandum from Richard L. Sneider to Dr. Kissinger, Top Secret/Declassified 5/2/12, June 23, 1969, NSC-Vietnam, Box 74, File 2, RMNPL.

38 Memorandum from Al Haig to Henry A. Kissinger, Top Secret/Declassified 8/7/03, June 24, 1969, Boc 710, File 1, RMNPL.

of Kent State, the White House intensified its attempts to open talks with China, beginning in September 1970.

During July 1971, U.S. secretary of state Henry Kissinger made a secret trip to Beijing to prepare for Nixon's trip the next year. On July 9, 1971, Kissinger and Zhou Enlai talked about cooperating against the real threat, the USSR: "PM Chou: I understand. There is another super-power. Dr. Kissinger: Here? To the North? PM Chou: Yes. We don't believe that super-power will be able to control the world. It will also be defeated as it stretches out its hand so far. You are feeling difficulties now, and they too will also feel difficulties. They are just following after you. Dr. Kissinger: With all respect, I think they triggered us, they caused our actions. Even today their constant probing makes it very hard to have a real settlement with them."[39]

* * *

In what must have seemed to many Chinese people as an American tributary mission, Nixon flew to Beijing in 1972 to meet with Mao Zedong. Washington and Beijing signed the *Shanghai Communiqué*, the first of three communiqués issued in 1972, 1979, and 1982 respectively. The *Shanghai Communiqué* provided two interpretations of the status of Taiwan. While China declared Taiwan to be one of its provinces, the United States agreed not to challenge the view shared by "all Chinese" on both sides of the Taiwan Strait that "there is but one China and that Taiwan is part of China."[40]

While Sino-U.S. diplomatic relations would not be fully reestablished until January 1, 1979, the long period of Sino-American estrangement had ended. On October 25, 1971, Taiwan lost its seat at the United Nations. Henceforth, the PRC sat on the Security Council as one of the five privileged nations to possess veto power, along with the USSR, the United States, France, and Great Britain, all victors at the end of World War II when the United Nations was established. When discussing their mutual dislike for the Soviet Union with Mao Zedong, Kissinger stated, "Mr. Chairman, it is really very important that we understand each other's motives. We will never knowingly

---

39 Memorandum of Conversation between Prime Minister Chou En-lai and Assistant to the President for National Security Affairs Henry A. Kissinger, July 9, 1971, Top Secret/Declassified, Box 846, File 1, RMNPL.

40 "Joint Communiqué," February 28, 1972, http://edition.cnn.com/SPECIALS/cold .war/episodes/15/documents/us.china/.

cooperate in an attack on China."[41] This diplomatic exchange was, in fact, a secret nonaggression pact between Washington and Beijing aimed at Moscow.

As a result of these secret talks between January 1972 and February 1973, the U.S. government promised Beijing to use its resources to "neutralize Soviet threats and deter threats against PRC," "oppose any attempt by the Soviet Union to engage in any aggressive action against China," and that in any U.S.-Soviet meetings, Washington would not "discuss its relations with the PRC without the PRC's knowledge or approval." Regarding Taiwan, the U.S. government agreed not to "support any Taiwan independence move-ment," it would remove two-thirds of its troops on Taiwan "as the problem in Southeast Asia is resolved," and the final one-third of U.S. troops would be removed "as progress is made on the peaceful resolution of the problem."[42] As for negotiations on the use of nuclear weapons, Washington promised Beijing that it "will never make secret arrangement. PRC will be informed. Anything will be public."[43]

As part of the new American alliance with China, the U.S. Navy also stepped aside and allowed the Chinese PLAN to take control of the Paracel Islands from South Vietnam during January 1974. This acquisition proved advantageous during the upcoming Sino-Vietnam War, since the PLAN's naval bases there kept Soviet warships in the region from helping North Vietnam. The PLAN simultaneously acted as a fleet-in-being exerting sea denial, plus guaranteed that unified Vietnam could not militarize these islands.

* * *

Nixon wanted to fulfill two main objectives: (1) extrication "with honor" from the Vietnam War and (2) victory in the Cold War. Secret diplomacy played a major role in achieving the first goal. During secret Moscow talks among Nixon, Brezhnev, and Kosygin in May 1972, Kosygin reassured Nixon, "There is not a single ship on the way to Vietnam now carrying mil-itary equipment—not one shell—only flour and foodstuffs, no armaments whatever." Cutting North Vietnam off from Soviet weapons was intended

41 Kissinger's discussion with Mao Zedong, NSC-HAK files, Box 98, February 17, 1973, RMNPL.

42 Memorandum from Winston Lord to HAK/HAIG, Top Secret/Sensitive Exclusively Eyes Only/Declassified, NSC-HAK files, March 17, 1972, Box 87, RMNPL; under-lining in the original document.

43 "Undertakings with the Chinese," Top Secret/Sensitive Exclusively Eyes Only/ Declassified, NSC-HAK files, February 1973, Box 87, RMNPL.

non-communist, that is their business.

Dr. Kissinger told me that if there was a peaceful settlement in Vietnam you would be agreeable to the Vietnamese doing whatever they want, having whatever they want after a period of time, say 18 months. If that is indeed true, and if the Vietnamese knew this, and it was true, they would be sympathetic on that basis. Even from the point of view of the election in the United States I submit that the end of the war at this particular time would play a positive role whereas escalation will not. As for sending in new waves of bombers against Vietnam, they cannot solve the problem and never can.

Document 8 Nixon, Brezhnev, and Kosygin Secret Agreement Ending the Vietnam War.

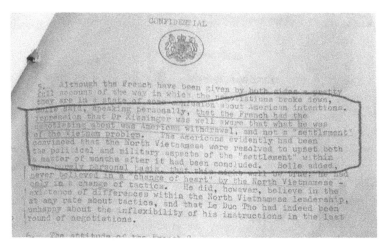

Document 9 British Document in the National Archives-UK Confirming this Secret Agreement.

to put pressure on Hanoi to come to terms with Washington. In return, the U.S. government made its own offer: If the USSR would help convince Hanoi to sign a peace agreement, preferably before Nixon's second term in office began, then after a certain amount of time—in this case 18 months—the U.S. government "would be agreeable to the Vietnamese doing whatever they want."[44] (Document 8) A British document in their National Archives confirmed this agreement. (Document 9)

During January 1973, the Paris Treaty formally ended the Vietnam War. Without Soviet backing, Hanoi had little choice but to open peace talks with the U.S. government. The peace agreement ending the Vietnam War was signed on January 27, 1973, just a week after Nixon was inaugurated for a second term.

---

44 Elleman, *The Impact of Coincidence*, 87–91.

States. I have wondered a good deal about whether or not we're
following the right course of action in killing as many North
Vietnamese as we're killing, because if Red China is a real
threat in the future then the most war-like people in Southeast Asia are the Vietnamese and I would be perfectly delighted
to see a lot of North Vietnamese in the way if Red China decided it was going to start to march.

Document 10 Clark M. Clifford Speech on 13 March 1969 Arguing a United Vietnam was Better for the United States.

Almost exactly a year and a half after the peace agreement went into effect during summer 1973, North Vietnam successfully invaded South Vietnam during spring 1975; as promised, the U.S. government did nothing to stop it.

As North Vietnam was invading South Vietnam during spring 1975, the U.S. ambassador in Saigon, Graham Martin, reported that Hanoi claimed it had a secret agreement with Washington, saying of North Vietnamese officials, "they would love to have you sit down with Le Duc Tho in order to confirm the rumors they are spreading through South Vietnam that this offensive is part of a deal they we have made with them." North Vietnamese officials even bragged about this secret agreement.[45]

The rapid collapse of South Vietnam appeared to take Washington by surprise, but the chaotic American withdrawal from Saigon was perhaps intended to cover up that a secret deal already existed. Strategically, it was better for Washington to have a united and strong Vietnam on China's southern border. On March 13, 1969, Clark M. Clifford, secretary of defense under Johnson, opined: "I have wondered a good deal about whether or not we're following the right course of action in killing as many North Vietnamese as we're killing, because if Red China is a real threat in the future then the most war-like people in Southeast Asia are the Vietnamese and I would be perfectly delighted to see a lot of North Vietnamese in the way if Red China decided it was going to start to march." In fact, Clifford persuasively argued that he did "not believe that the conflict today in South Vietnam involves the national security of the United States."[46] (Document 10)

---

45 Ibid.

46 "Remarks of Honorable Clark M. Clifford Before The Council on Foreign Relations," Thursday, March 13, 1969, New York City, citing National Security Council (NSC)— Vietnam, Box 68, file 6, 36, RMNPL.

Washington's expectations that a united Vietnam would halt Chinese expansion southward were soon rewarded. In September 1975, China's attempt to push Vietnam into an alliance backfired: "The breakdown of Vietnam's relations with China after 1975 and Vietnam's current pro-Soviet alignment may be traced to Vietnamese resistance to Chinese pressures to take sides."[47] When Hanoi resisted, Beijing threatened it with severe consequences, including during 1976, when "China recalled several groups of specialists from Vietnam and delayed work on a number of projects being built with Chinese aid."[48]

* * *

By the summer of 1978, Sino-Soviet tensions had further intensified, as reflected by increased Soviet troop concentrations along China's border. During September 1978, the USSR increased arms shipments to Vietnam, both by air and by sea. These included "aircraft, missiles, tanks, and munitions."[49] This culminated on November 2, 1978, when the two countries signed a Treaty of Friendship and Cooperation. This agreement was clearly aimed at China, since one clause stated that Vietnam and the USSR would "immediately consult each other" if either was "attacked or threatened with attack [...] with a view to eliminating that threat."[50] Reportedly, a secret protocol also granted Soviet military forces access to Vietnam's "airfields and ports."[51]

Vietnam used its treaty with Russia to pressure China, while Beijing tried to outflank them both by opening relations with Washington. On December 15, 1978, China announced that Sino-American relations would be normalized on January 1, 1979. Soon afterward, Vietnam attacked Cambodia, and by January 7, 1979, Vietnamese forces had secured Phnom Penh. The timing of the Moscow-Hanoi treaty and Beijing's new alliance with Washington were linked: "Thus two strategic alliances had been created in the closing

---

47 Ramesh Thaku and Carlyle Thayer, *Soviet Relations with India and Vietnam* (New York: St. Martin's Press, 1992), 287.

48 Stephen J. Morris, *Why Vietnam Invaded Cambodia: Political Culture and the Causes of War* (Stanford, CA: Stanford University Press, 1999), 174.

49 Robert S. Ross, *The Indochina Tangle* (New York: Columbia University Press, 1988), 208.

50 *FBIS SU*, November 6, 1978, 6–9.

51 Thaku and Thayer, *Soviet Relations with India and Vietnam*, 61.

months of 1978, a Soviet-Vietnamese alliance and a Sino-American alliance, and they would prevail for about a decade."[52]

China's 1979 invasion of Vietnam was also a response to Hanoi's treaty with Moscow. Deng Xiaoping stated that the 1978 Soviet-Vietnamese "military alliance" was really just part of the USSR's long-time goal to "encircle China." In the wake of Vietnam's successful occupation of Cambodia, it was "the resultant Soviet encirclement of China [that] necessitated a limited invasion of Vietnam."[53] According to King C. Chen, "had there been no Soviet-Vietnamese alliance, the sixteen-day war between China and Vietnam might not have been fought."[54] When Moscow warned Beijing that it might intervene, China ignored this warning.

Beijing announced it would invade Vietnam on February 15, 1979—the very first day that it could legally terminate the 1950 Sino-Soviet Treaty of Friendship, Alliance, and Mutual Assistance—and attacked Vietnam two days later. China's PLA forces invading Vietnam eventually totaled almost a quarter million troops, but the Vietnamese adopted guerrilla tactics to rob China of a quick victory. When Moscow did not intervene, however, Beijing publicly proclaimed that the USSR had broken its promise to assist Vietnam and announced its intention to withdraw its troops on March 5, 1979, on the 26th anniversary of Stalin's death in 1953.

To many commentators, China's attack appeared to fail, since Vietnam's military potential was not seriously damaged and its invasion of Cambodia had not been reversed. But if the real goal behind China's attack was to expose Soviet assurances of military support as a fraud, then China's attack was a strategic success. The USSR's failure to support Vietnam thus emboldened China to announce on April 3, 1979, that it would terminate the 30-year Sino-Soviet Treaty the next year. The Sino-Soviet alliance was now officially over, allowing China to shift toward the United States. Moscow's refusal to intervene in the Sino-Vietnamese War also effectively terminated the Soviet-Vietnamese military pact. Beijing achieved a strategic victory by eliminating any future chance of a two-front war.

As Deng Xiaoping had announced from the very beginning, China conducted a limited action against Vietnam. The "Chinese demonstrated that

---

52 Ramses Amer, "Sino-Vietnamese Normalization in the Light of the Crisis of the Late 1970s," *Pacific Affairs*, Vol. 67, No. 3 (fall 1994), 362–363.

53 Ross, *The Indochina Tangle*, 217, 225.

54 King C. Chen, *China's War with Vietnam, 1979* (Stanford, CA: Hoover Institution Press, 1987), 27.

they could attack a Soviet ally without retaliation from the 'paper polar bear'."[55] Many of China's best troops were stationed far to the north along the Sino-Soviet border, plus even though the Soviet Navy outmatched the PLAN, there was no open Chinese conflict with Soviet vessels.[56] Chinese military forces in the Paracels provided not only an "outpost" to watch the Soviets from but also a buffer area plus "fleet-in-being" between the PRC and Vietnam. The islands also acted as a strategic "area to stage punitive naval strikes against the Vietnamese."[57]

Beijing's withdrawal announcement on March 5, 1979, indicated that it felt it had "punished" Hanoi sufficiently during its limited attack, even while proving to the world that Moscow was too weak to intervene on the side of an ally. Vietnam was "chastened by the experience of 1979, [and] now stations 700,000 combat troops in the northern portion of the country."[58] When Sino-Vietnamese peace talks opened during April 1979, China demanded that Vietnam recognize the PRC's sovereignty in the South China Sea, in particular over the Paracels, but Hanoi rejected this proposal.[59] After proving that Moscow would not intervene on Hanoi's behalf, Beijing voided the 1950 Sino-Soviet Treaty in April 1980. As a result, even though Sino-Soviet negotiations were officially opened again during October 1979, the Soviet invasion of Afghanistan gave China a pretense for calling off all future meetings, thereby precluding the negotiation of any new Sino-Soviet diplomatic treaty.

* * *

President Jimmy Carter and Chairman Deng Xiaoping opened relations between the United States and China on January 1, 1979. The normalization of U.S.-Chinese relations was endorsed at the Guadeloupe Summit by the British, French, and West Germans. Washington's European allies, plus Asian allies like Japan, viewed positively increased scientific and technological

55 Banning Garrett, "The Strategic Triangle and the Indochina Crisis," in David W.P. Elliott, Ed., *The Third Indochina Conflict* (Boulder, Colorado: Westview Press, 1981), 212.

56 Edward C. O'Dowd, *Chinese Military Strategy in the Third Indochina War: The last Maoist war* (London: Routledge Press, 2007), 66.

57 Steven J. Hood, *Dragons Entangled: Indochina and the China-Vietnam War* (Armonk, NY: M.E. Sharpe, 1992), 129.

58 Karl D. Jackson, "Indochina, 1982-1985: Peace Yields to War," in Richard H. Solomon and Masataka Kosaka, Eds., *The Soviet Far East Military Buildup* (Dover, MA: Auburn House Publishing Company, 1986), 206.

59 Hemen Ray, *China's Vietnam War* (New Delhi: Radiant Publishers, 1983), 116.

exchanges with the PRC. Providing the PRC with high-technology goods would put Moscow on "notice that provocative Soviet behavior could stimulate increasingly intimate Sino-US ties with security overtones."[60]

Due to the chaos of the Cultural Revolution, China was at least 10–20 years behind the West. The U.S. government knew that "the Chinese saw an urgent need to obtain foreign technology both to build their economy, which had suffered not only from years of domestic turmoil but also from the cutoff of Soviet assistance, and to increase their defense capabilities." In particular, "Computer and petroleum technology head the list of imports the Chinese want from the US to accelerate their modernization efforts."[61]

This Sino-American technology transfer arrangement helped Beijing obtain goods normally put off-limits to Communist countries by COCOM. Carter ordered increased technology transfers to create a "strong and secure China." His four goals were to create a China that (1) "remains basically self-sufficient in agriculture and does not become a major claimant on world food supplies in the decades ahead"; (2) "remains self-sufficient and even a contributor to world natural resource supplies, particularly in the energy realm"; (3) "remains confident it can deter a Sino-Soviet conflict and retains the capacity to delineate an independent foreign policy"; and (4) "develops an S&T manpower pool from among its ample and talented populace to enable China to contribute to the solution of the global problem which will increasingly confront us." The ultimate goal was to have China "play a central role in the maintenance of the global equilibrium."[62] A November 20, 1978, meeting of the East-West Planning Group had noted how Soviet leaders were "unusually irritated [...] [by] a pattern of events, notably arms deals with Europeans, that aim toward a more substantial security relationship between China and the West."[63]

In response to the Soviet invasion of Afghanistan in December 1979, COCOM retaliated by tightening controls on the USSR.[64] Carter instructed

---

60 "Sino-US Scientific & Technological Cooperation: A Political Overview," September 29, 1978, Secret (declassified on 5/17/1996), NSA (6) Brzezinski Material, Country, Box 8, Jimmy Carter Presidential Library (JCPL).

61 "An Overview of Chinese Foreign Policy," undated, Secret (declassified on 12/15/2010), NSA (5) Brzezinski Material VIP Box 2, JCPL.

62 "I. Current S&T Exchanges with the PRC," June 30, 1978, Confidential (declassified on 5/17/1996), NSA (6) Brzezinski Material, Country, Box 8, JCPL.

63 Memo from Fritz Ermarth to Zbigniew Brzezinski entitled "East-West Planning Group Discussion on Sino-Soviet Relations," November 20, 1978, Secret/Sensitive GDS (declassified on 5/17/1996), NSA (6) Brzezinski Material, Country, Box 8, JCPL.

64 Memorandum from Christine Dobson to Peter Tarnoff entitled "COCOM: Exceptions Procedure for China," March 3, 1980, Confidential (declassified on 10/25/2012), NSA (6) Brzezinski Material, Country, Box 9, JCPL.

the secretary of commerce to move China from "Country Group Y to a separate category with its own letter designation." According to a confidential memorandum: "Since it is not US policy to treat China and the USSR the same for export control purposes, it is misleading to have them share the same Country Group in the export control regulations."[65] This decision opened the door for selling China jet engines and naval equipment. When Vice Foreign Minister Geng Biao visited the United States during May 1980, he was initially told that "his request for jet engines for China's military aircraft" would be rejected.[66] But as time went on, these strict technological "red lines" were often pushed and sometimes crossed. For example, the British plan to sell eight to twelve Olympus engines (two per ship) to China was a test case. So as to not involve COCOM, the U.S. government told Britain it "would recommend the British bypass COCOM in this instance." Furthermore, it requested: "We would prefer the British not to indicate either to the Chinese or the Soviets that we had been consulted."[67]

*   *   *

The U.S. government's decision to sell dual-use equipment to China's military was critical to winning the Cold War. Michel Oksenberg even told Brzezinski: "As to China's efforts to modernize its military forces, we believe that selective improvement of China's military capabilities may actually be in our interest, since we desire the Chinese to retain confidence in their ability to deter a Sino-Soviet conflict."[68] Oksenberg reported that within China, their focus was on the Army, Air Force, and Navy, in that order.[69] During a trip

---

65 Memorandum from Zbigniew Brzezinski to the Secretary of Commerce, March 17, 1980, Confidential (declassified on 10/25/2012), NSA (6) Brzezinski Material, Country, Box 9, JCPL.
66 Memorandum from Roger W. Sullivan to Zbigniew Brzezinski entitled "Your Meeting with Chinese Foreign Minister Geng Biao," May 28, 1980, Secret (declassified on 10/29/2015), NSA (6) Brzezinski Material, Country, Box 10, JCPL.
67 Memorandum for the Secretary of Defense, entitled "British Sale of Marine Engines to the People's Republic of China," undated, Secret (declassified on 6/11/2013), NSA (6) Brzezinski Material, Country, Box 8, JCPL.
68 Memorandum from Michel Oksenberg to Zbigniew Brzezinski, "Briefing of the President on Chinese Internal Affairs and Aspects of Our China Policy," February 28, 1978, Secret (declassified on 5/17/1996), NSA (6) Brzezinski Material, Country, Box 8, JCPL; all underlining in the original document.
69 Memorandum from Michel Oksenberg to Zbigniew Brzezinski entitled "China Visit by National Defense University," June 18, 1979, Confidential (declassified on 2/1/2012), NSA (6) Brzezinski Material, Country, Box 9, JCPL.

to China by Secretary of Defense Harold Brown, the Chinese gave him a list of items: "It was implied that these items would be for military use."[70] All of this equipment was years, perhaps decades, ahead of the technology China was using at the time. These technology transfers sent a potent message to Moscow.

The weakest part of China's military was its Navy, so there was little immediate downside to selling strategic dual-use naval technology to China.[71] After a U.S. military delegation went to China during September 1980, William Odom reported on China's Navy: "They are extremely modest, more so than any other military technology. Some of the basic shipbuilding techniques for hulls are quite good, but that won't yield a significant naval force." Based on what they saw in China, "Even Admiral Monroe (the Navy was thought to be the most reluctant) decided that we should get on with military assistance in the middle level technology as soon as possible." Odom was particularly concerned that Washington not "compromise a lot of sensitive technology without achieving any significant upgrade in the Chinese military posture."[72]

On January 4, 1980, Carter decided, "We are now prepared to consider sale of military equipment, but not arms, to China on a carefully selected case-by-cases basis."[73] By January 10, 1980, Frank Press reported to Carter that a number of science and technology agreements had been signed with China, including "ten protocols for cooperation in specific areas such as space, student exchanges, agriculture, high energy physics, R&D management, atmospheric sciences, oceanography, and health. The most recent protocol was the one on hydro-electric power signed by the Vice President during his visit to China."[74]

---

70 Memorandum from Nicholas Platt, et al, to the Secretary of Defense entitled "Technology Transfers and Military Equipment Sales to China," February 26, 1980, Confidential (declassified on 12/5/2011), NSA (6) Brzezinski Material, Country, Box 9, JCPL.
71 Memorandum from William E. Odom to Zbigniew Brzezinski entitled "My Trip to the PRC with Perry's Military Technology Delegation," September 22, 1980, Secret (declassified on 8/10/2010), NSA (6) Brzezinski Material, Country, Box 10, JCPL.
72 Memorandum from William E. Odom to Zbigniew Brzezinski entitled "My Trip to the PRC with Perry's Military Technology Delegation," September 22, 1980, Secret (declassified on 8/10/2010), NSA (6) Brzezinski Material, Country, Box 10, JCPL.
73 Memorandum from Richard Holbrooke, Nicholas Platt, and Michel Oksenberg to the Secretary of State, the Secretary of Defense, and to Dr. Zbigniew Brzezinski entitled "Sale of Sensitive Equipment to China," January 22, 1980, Top Secret (declassified on 2/11/1999), Brzezinski Donated, Subject, Box 34, JCPL.
74 Memorandum from Frank Press to the President entitled "Meeting on US-China S&T Relations," January 10, 1980, Confidential (declassified on 3/12/2013), NSA (6) Brzezinski Material, Country, Box 9, JCPL.

Beijing was particularly interested in acquiring military equipment and dual-use technology like aeronautics and electronics, which had military applications. On May 23, 1980, a Secret NSC Memorandum noted about a forthcoming visit by Geng Biao: "Regarding military equipment, [...] we have approved export applications submitted by U.S. industry for airborne tactical radars, early warning radars, Chinook (CH-47) helicopters, truck tractors, a tropospheric communications system and a secure communications system. We are also working to add the C-130 to this list."[75]

* * *

The differential sanctions changed radically after the opening of U.S.-Chinese diplomatic relations on January 1, 1979, and especially after the Soviet invasion of Afghanistan. In July 1980, new China export control guidelines were approved, including not to deny sales where the end-user was "engaged in military activities," and the Department of Commerce was told to "give priority attention to processing the backlog of cases for China."[76] At that point, 60 cases were awaiting action.[77] The Carter Administration's long-term goals in opening science and technology exchanges with the PRC were clear: "Since 1971, the United States has sought a better relationship with both Moscow and Peking than they have with each other." Another major goal of the "S&T exchanges as in other realms of activity, is to enmesh China more fully in the international system."[78]

To expedite these technology transfers to China, on June 25, 1981, the incoming Ronald Reagan Administration listed as a significant strategic success the fact: "We have liberalized export control policy for the PRC making available a wider range of technology. This has put the US on the forefront of China's drive for modernization. China has been removed from

---

75 Memorandum from Ben Huberman and Roger Sullivan to Zbigniew Brzezinski entitled "Military and Dual-Use Exports to China," May 23, 1980, Secret (declassified on 3/30/1999), NSA Staff, Far East, Box 70, JCPL.

76 Memorandum from Zbigniew Brzezinski to Secretary of State, Secretary of Defense, and Secretary of Commerce, July 21, 1980, Confidential (declassified on 8/25/2009), NSA (6) Brzezinski Material, Country, Box 10, JCPL.

77 Memorandum from Roger W. Sullivan and Ben Huberman to Zbigniew Brzezinski entitled "Your Call to Secretary Klutznick—Talking Points," July 18, 1980, NSA (6) Brzezinski Material, Country, Box 10, JCPL.

78 "I. Current S&T Exchanges with the PRC," June 30, 1978, Confidential (declassified on 5/17/1996), NSA (6) Brzezinski Material, Country, Box 8, JCPL.

the munitions control list."[79] During June 1983, China became a "friendly, non-allied country" and was shifted into export control "Country Group V." Technical guidelines, called "green lines," were created that included products for routine approval for export to China by COCOM.[80]

By 1985, COCOM was facing a "near-crushing caseload" of over 4,400 exception requests, fully 3,500 of them from U.S. exporters. So, COCOM created "Administrative Exceptions Notes (AEN) for China in 27 entries of COCOM's dual use control list."[81] China's naval purchases were huge, including buying in 1985 alone the *Phalanx* ship defense system, towed array sonars, *Mark 46* torpedoes, *Hawk* air defense missiles, and *TOW* anti-armor missiles, to name just a few.[82]

Because of dual-use technology sales to China, the COCOM strategic export mechanism was soon stretched to its limit. There were even discussions about getting rid of COCOM export controls altogether for China. After 1985, these controls were streamlined further, which "reduced significantly the China caseload in COCOM and sped up licensing of high-technology exports to China by the US and other COCOM members."[83] The AENs (Administrative Exception Notes) gradually increased to 39 categories, and the number of U.S. exports requiring COCOM review dropped from 50 percent to 9 percent, or in 1988, just over "500 of the approximately 800 China cases submitted to COCOM."[84]

By May 1986, China's technology requests were being evaluated more rapidly, and 12 were approved. One, an IBM Digital Processor, was the "largest computer exported to China" and was not being sold to either the USSR or to Eastern Europe. Other approvals included a Seismic Data Recording System, a Magnetron Sputtering device, a CGA Photorepeater Exposure System, an Eaton Medium Current Ion Implantation System, and a Quatred Corp Model 1010 (X) Xenon Laser, to name just a few. The only Chinese request denied outright was a 5751-A Compact Range and 2083 Antenna Test System.[85]

* * *

79 John Poindexter, Foreign/Defense Issues and Objectives, RAC Box 1, June 25, 1981, Ronald Reagan Presidential Library (RRPL).
80 Daniel Levin, NSC, GS OF 73, George H. W. Bush Presidential Library (GHWBPL).
81 Douglas Paal, 1989-90, China Files, G 28 SF 73, GHWBPL.
82 "U.S. Options for Responding to the Slaughter in China," *Asian Studies Center: Backgrounder*, No. 92, June 7, 1989, The Heritage Foundation.
83 Daniel Levin, NSC, GS OF 73, GHWBPL.
84 Douglas Paal, 1989-90, China Files, G 28 SF 73, GHWBPL.
85 Donald Gregg, "Meeting with Foreigners, 1986," 15-16 May 1986, 19816, 28 G, GHWBPL.

Washington's strategic goal was to pull China away from the Soviet bloc
and closer to the Western democratic-capitalist countries. Carter was a retired
U.S. Navy submariner, so building up China's Navy was a high priority. But
selling Beijing advanced military equipment was a risky policy. Secretary of
State Cyrus Vance even warned Carter against "a military security relationship with China," since to enter into a China pact would sacrifice critical
leverage over the USSR intended to "moderate Soviet behavior" and thereby
"lose us the leverage the China factor now gives us. The China card, once
played, loses its inhibiting effect."[86]

Carter Administration officials repeatedly warned that rapid Chinese
military advances could threaten the United States. Odom said, "Nor should
we forget that we are dealing with a brutal regime [...]. As charming as the
Chinese are to us, we should never lose sight of the fact that our help is much
more in their interest than it is in our interest. I am worried that they will be
much better at organizing to keep leverage over us than we will be at gaining
leverage over them in a military relationship." He cautioned: "We had better
take some lessons from previous efforts in technology transfers and organize
ourselves so that we control the process at the policy level. We should not
repeat what we did with the Soviets in the early 1970s and what we are doing
with Saudi Arabia now."[87]

Warnings also came from Australian official Paul Dibb, who had lunch
on January 31, 1979, with a group of Soviet officials visiting Canberra. One
official named Nayanov openly acknowledged that a technology transfer program to China would "pose a major, long-term threat to the USSR about
15 years from now."[88] On July 2, 1981, a Soviet note further warned of the
"dangerous consequences of that the policy of encouraging the expansionist
aspiration of China might have for the peace and stability in the Far East
and South-East Asia."[89] These Soviet warnings were eerily similar to a 1978
Washington report that said, "We have no interest in China's acquisition

---

86 Memorandum from Cyrus Vance to the President, September 18, 1979, Top Secret
   Eyes Only (declassified on 10/1/2008), NSA (6) Brzezinski Material, Country, Box
   9, JCPL.
87 Memorandum from William E. Odom to Zbigniew Brzezinski entitled "My Trip to
   the PRC with Perry's Military Technology Delegation," September 22, 1980, Secret
   (declassified on 8/10/2010), NSA (6) Brzezinski Material, Country, Box 10, JCPL;
   underlining in the original.
88 Meeting Report by Paul Dibb, Canberra, January 31, 1979, UKNA, FCO 21/1703.
89 Richard Pipes, Files, Chron 07/02/1981-07/07/1981, July 2, 1981, Box 10, Secret/
   Sensitive (declassified on 6/20/08), RRPL.

of technology and equipment that would destabilize the delicate balance of power in the Western Pacific."[90]

During July 1981, the State Department's Briefing Paper stressed: "Our strategic relationship with China is important to the global balance of power. We intend to expand our bilateral ties through liberalized technology transfer guidelines, increased commercial exchanges, and greater defense cooperation."[91] But on September 22, 1981, Reagan also signed an additional National Security Decision focusing high-tech sales to China on just those items that "should not contribute significantly to improvements in Chinese offensive and power-projection capabilities."[92] Regardless, some 40 years later, the U.S. Navy is facing a growing naval threat in the Western Pacific that is, to a large degree, a "Frankensteinian Monster" of its own making.

* * *

By 1989, the Cold War was widely considered to be over. The U.S. government's strategy of selling high-technology weapons to China had worked. The Soviet government under Mikhail Gorbachev was unable to adopt domestic reforms sufficient to keep up. After the June 4, 1989, Tiananmen Massacre, Washington immediately suspended its Munitions List cases in COCOM. On June 4, 1989, General Counsel Jerome H. Silber recommended the immediate suspension of all Foreign Military Sales programs to China.[93] Thereafter, on June 27, 1989, the members voted: "The procedure established in COCOM Doc Reg CH (89) will remain unchanged and thus exception requests will continue to be reviewed case by case, on the basis of COCOM's strategic criteria."[94]

Faced with enormous public revulsion at China's massacre of defenseless students, Washington told Beijing that all future export sales can only be made "if the proposed export is for commercial use and therefore consistent with President George H. W. Bush's desire to maintain the commercial relationship" with China.[95] On May 11, 1990, Brent Scowcroft presented a memo

90 "I. Current S&T Exchanges with the PRC," June 30, 1978, Confidential (declassified on 5/17/1996), NSA (6) Brzezinski Material, Country, Box 8, JCPL.
91 Donald Gregg, July 1981, Foreign Policy—General [3], OA/ID 19856-012, GHWBPL.
92 Donald Gregg, National Security Decision Directive Number 11, September 22, 1981, Country 1983: China 19 G, GHWBPL.
93 Douglas Paal, NSC, China [2], GS OF 73, GHWBPL.
94 Douglas Paal, 1989-90, China Files, G 28 SF 73, GHWBPL.
95 Ibid.

to Bush on the suspension of high-technology exports to China, including all Munitions List cases. He concluded that "no incremental or policy liberation of COCOM [...] is currently under consideration" and that "over the long term, the lack of export control liberalization could have a significant impact on China's ability to upgrade its technological base, promote the growth of industry and agriculture, and become competitive in global markets."[96]

In other words, no more special treatment for China. Beijing was not standing still, however. During April 1990, "a delegation from [Soviet aircraft company] Antonov's Design Bureau had visited China to discuss Sino-Soviet aircraft cooperation, the first major visit of a Soviet aviation delegation to China in 30 years," which "accurately reflects a Chinese decision to more aggressively play the field and avoid being boxed in by the US—or any other single supplier—in the future."[97] In October 1992, one critic on the National Security Council called it "unrealistic" that China would not buy more Soviet SU-27 "Flanker" planes and further warned that "acquisition of a fourth-generation air superiority fighter without AAMS would be pointless."[98] During this period, Sino-U.S. technology transfers virtually ended.

*   *   *

Throughout the 1980s, the U.S. government used dual-use technology transfers to China to put extreme military and economic pressure on the USSR. It worked. The Cold War ended on Western terms. By 1994, the last Russian troops had pulled completely out of Germany. Meanwhile, the Tiananmen Massacre resulted in a steep reduction of U.S. high-tech exports to China, in particular military sales. Washington soon adopted a new strategy for Eastern Europe. During June 1990, Robert Gates reported on critical changes in the COCOM structure impacting Russia and Eastern Europe: "We have taken a bold step to revitalize COCOM, make controls realistic, and open the way for modernization of Eastern Europe."[99]

COCOM sales to China continued to drop while high-technology sales to Eastern Europe soared. Following the USSR's total collapse in December 1991, a White House press release from June 17, 1992, stated that a new "COCOM Forum" would (1) increase access for Russia and the other former Soviet republics to "advanced Western goods and technology," (2) set up

---

96 Karl Jackson, China-General, BPR NSC Files, G 28 SF 73, GHWBPL.
97 Douglas Paal, 1989-90, China Files, G 28 SF 73, GHWBPL.
98 Memorandum on PRC Flanker ACQ, Secret (Declassified in part 7/23/15), November 2, 1992, Lehr, Deborah, NSC, GS OF 73, GHWBPL.
99 Robert L. Hutchings, May 1990-June 1990, GS OF 73, Box 3, Stack 6, GHWBPL.

procedures to ensure "against diversion of these sensitive items to military or other unauthorized users," and (3) support "further cooperation on matters of common concern on export controls."[100]

The sanctions program created in the early 1950s continued all the way through until the end of the Cold War and beyond. Soon after the Tiananmen Massacre, however, the focus changed: in just three years, the COCOM-regulated differential sanctions reversed from full support for China and maximum pressure on the USSR to the opposite stance of restricting arms sales to China. This reversal demonstrated just how versatile the differential sanctions program was to changing political circumstances within the former Communist Bloc countries. Thus, the sanctions program proved critical to winning the Cold War.

---

100 CO165 Russia, GHWBPL.

CONCLUSION: THE COLD WAR'S STRATEGIC SIGNIFICANCE TODAY

The ABCs of Cold War History: Anglo-America, Bloc Sovietique, China, 1919–1994 shows how China was at the very heart of the Cold War. It was the biggest prize for the West, since China alone tied up 25 percent of the Soviet armed forces. Between NATO on the West and China on the East, the USSR was completely hemmed in. This pincer movement contributed to Soviet over-extension in Afghanistan and reverses in Eastern Europe, culminating in the fall of the Berlin Wall, the end of the Cold War, and—two years after that—the total collapse of the USSR. The Evil Empire was gone. By 1994, the last Russian troops had vacated Germany. These historic events showed that the unprecedented Anglo-American-China alliance had achieved a complete victory. The Cold War ended on Western, not Soviet, terms.

Winning the Cold War was well worth the huge investment of time and money. However, there were many potential downsides, including the long-term military effect of the technology transfer program to China. This program helped create new threats to the West, including encouraging the emergence of an imperialist China intent on satisfying its historical ambitions to dominate Southeast Asia. (See Map 5.) Interestingly, on April 10, 1974, Deng Xiaoping foresaw this possible danger when he told a special session of the United Nations General Assembly: "If one day China should change her colour and turn into a Superpower, if she too should play the tyrant in the world, and everywhere subject others to her bullying, aggression and exploitation, the peoples of the world should identify her as social-imperialist, expose it and work together with the Chinese people to overthrow it."[1] One Soviet official even warned that the technology transfer program to China might "also encourage the emergence of a China which could use

---

1 Deng Xiaoping, Speech to the Special Session of the United Nations General Assembly, April 10, 1974, CO-34 General 9/1/77-12/12//78, JCPL.

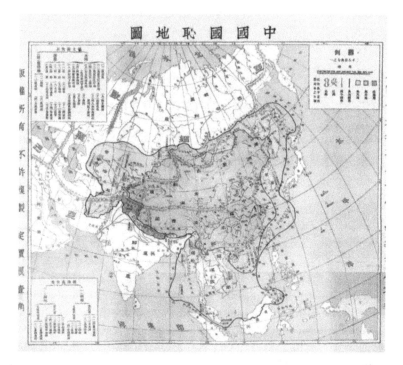

Map 5 Map of China's national humiliation (1927). Source: "Zhonghua guochi ditu, zaiban" (Shanghai: Zhonghua Shuju, 1927). This translates as "Map of China's National Humiliation, Reprint." This map is held by the Chinese University of Hong Kong.

its enhanced military power to satisfy its historical ambitions to dominate South-East Asia."[2] A half-century later, America and its sea power allies are even now facing just such a resurgent China.

The strategic steps to winning the Cold War included: (1) letting the Chinese Communists take all of Mainland China in 1949; (2) Nationalist Blockade; (3) Taiwan Patrol Force; (4) Strategic Embargo; (5) China Differential; (6) helping create the Sino-Soviet split; (7) the Vietnam War dividing the Sino-Soviet monolith by means of the SAM soaking strategy; (8) the outbreak of the Sino-Soviet War of 1969; (9) Nixon "Flipping" China; (10) China's 1974 invasion of the Paracel Islands; (11) the unification of Vietnam, the Soviet-Vietnamese alliance, and the January 1, 1979 Sino-American alliance; (12) the 1979 Sino-Vietnamese War canceling the 30-year Sino-Soviet Friendship Treaty; (13) the creation of Carter's Navy with the ultimate goal of forging an East-West

2 Meeting Report by Paul Dibb, Canberra, January 31, 1979, FCO 21/1703, TNA/UK.

pincer aimed at the USSR; and (14) the Big Squeeze from both China and NATO that eventually destroyed the USSR.

This was the 14-point strategy that "won" the Cold War. The war's aftermath then created five new factors: (A) China now has the world's biggest navy; (B) A fully united Vietnam can better stand up to China; (C) A China torn by competing land and sea commitments; (D) The historical and strategic importance of Sino-Russian relations; and (E) The continued applicability of these 14 points to winning Cold War II.

*   *   *

(A) Competition over winning China was at the heart of the Cold War. Truman and Eisenhower used the Nationalist blockade, the Taiwan Patrol, the strategic embargo, and the China differential to push Russia and China closer together and create a split. It was then Johnson's strategy of using SAM baiting during the Vietnam War to break apart the Sino-Soviet alliance. When combined with the Nixon-Brezhnev secret agreement ending the Vietnam War and creating a unified Vietnam, that made the creation of an East-West pincer against Russia possible. These diplomatic victories may have been the one-two punch that ultimately destroyed the USSR.

After Nixon "flipped" China in 1972 and Carter and Deng allied more closely on January 1, 1979, the U.S. government used high-technology dual-use transfers to help build up a strong China, both economically and militarily. This technology transfer strategy put additional pressure on an already overextended Soviet military. Reagan then added his own touch when a "Secret" Export Control Policy was adopted on June 8, 1981: "Our strategic interests dictate the preservation of China as an effective counterweight to growing Soviet military power."[3] During July 1981, a State Department Briefing Paper even stressed: "Our strategic relationship with China is important to the global balance of power. We intend to expand our bilateral ties through liberalized technology transfer guidelines, increased commercial exchanges, and greater defense cooperation."[4] James Lilly further noted that China tied up "25% of Soviet armed forces."[5]

Sea power is the key to global prosperity. With American technical assistance, the PLAN was able to make enormous strides during the 1980s.

---

3 George A. Keyworth, Presidential Directives on Export Control Policy to China, June 8, 1981, RAC Box 13, RRPL.

4 Donald Gregg, July 1981, Foreign Policy—General [3], OA/ID 19856-012, GHWBPL.

5 James Lilly, Memorandum to MGEN Robert L. Schweitzer, NSC, April 21, 1981, Box 1, RRPL.

Technological leaps in radar, missiles, and communications put extreme pressure on the USSR, helping to precipitate its collapse. After the Cold War ended, Beijing quickly transitioned away from buying Western military equipment to purchasing Soviet-era military technology. In 1992, China bought the *Varyag* aircraft carrier from the newly independent Ukraine; renamed *Liaoning*, it became the first of what would become a small fleet of Chinese aircraft carriers. China now has the world's largest navy in terms of the number of ships. But as the Russian-Ukrainian War has shown, the Soviet-era military technology that China so eagerly purchased is far inferior to those Western high-tech exports that Beijing was denied access to after the June 4, 1989, Tiananmen Massacre.

*   *   *

(B) Unlike before, China also now faces a unified Vietnam, which better serves U.S. national and strategic interests. Clark Clifford's March 13, 1969, talk argued that a strong Vietnam could better contain Beijing by acting as a potent barrier opposing China's southward expansion. International law is also being used to try to rein in Beijing's imperialist ambitions. On July 12, 2016, the Permanent Court of Arbitration (PCA) ruled in favor of the Philippines when it concluded: "certain sea areas are within the exclusive economic zone of the Philippines, because those areas are not overlapped by any possible entitlement of China."[6] Beijing's open rejection of the PCA decision, however, has "increased tensions in the South China Sea and delayed both co-operation and progress towards an agreed Code of Conduct."[7]

As part of its aggressive military strategy, Beijing has used a number of South China Sea islands, including the Paracels following its successful 1974 invasion, to base fleets-in-being, air forces, and missiles to enforce sea denial strategies. This worked well in the 1979 Sino-Vietnamese War, successfully keeping the Soviet Navy at bay. But if used in a contemporary war, such sea denial strategies will carry the additional second-order risk of skyrocketing insurance rates that might halt not just targeted traffic but all commercial

---

6 Matikas Santos, "Philippines Wins Arbitration Case v. China over South China Sea," *Inquirer.net*, July 12, 2016, http://globalnation.inquirer.net/140358/philippines -arbitration-decision-maritime-dispute-south-china-sea-arbitral-tribunal-unclos-itlos [accessed November 29, 2016]; citing *South China Sea Arbitration (Philippines v. China)*, Award of July 12, 2016.

7 Sam Bateman, "The Impact of the Arbitration Case on Regional Maritime Security," in Wu Shicun and Keyuan Zou, Eds., *Arbitration Concerning the South China Sea: Philippines versus China* (Surrey: Ashgate, 2016), 239.

traffic through contested waters. A resource-dependent China would be the biggest loser if such an escalation were to take place in the South China Sea.

Although the Chinese military has made enormous strides recently, during an actual war, the PLAN might face crippling losses. The outcome of any naval conflict will depend on high levels of command-and-control, interoperability of equipment both on a single ship and among different ships within the same fleet, and jointness not only between different services but, more importantly, within the three Chinese regional fleets, as well as on the quality of the training and education received by the Chinese naval personnel. Unless these challenges are overcome, the PLAN can never compete as a peer with the world's other great navies, no matter how many ships it builds.

* * *

(C) China has long been considered to be one of the world's greatest continental powers. The Great Wall is often cited as proof of China's traditional focus on land power. Chinese warfare was also mainly land warfare; Sun Tzu's *Art of War* discussed how river currents could impact military strategy, but there was no mention of warfare on oceans. Throughout its long history, therefore, China focused mainly on the land. Attempts to become a sea power previously all failed. China's ambitions during the early Ming dynasty saw heightened maritime activity from 1405–1435, as Ming China ruled as the supreme sea power over Asia. Ming Treasure Fleets reached as far as East Africa. But in 1449, the Ming suffered a disastrous land defeat at the hands of their erstwhile enemy, the Mongols. This forced a reallocation of military resources away from the sea to the land.

In a similar manner to the early Ming, China's shift from being a land power to a sea power has recently sped up: as of 2019, the PLAN became the largest navy in the world with over 300 ships, almost two dozen more than the U.S. Navy, although the U.S. Navy ships are heavier. As a direct result of its modernization efforts, the PLAN has become better equipped to face up to its geographic responsibilities, especially in the Western Pacific. These include territorial disputes over the Senkaku/Diaoyu islands with Japan, rising tensions over the Taiwan Strait, and disputed sovereignty over the South China Sea.

China has been adopting a more aggressive maritime policy in the South China Sea and elsewhere. In response, many of China's maritime neighbors are increasing cooperation with Japan, India, Australia, and the United States (the so-called "Quad") to act as a counterweight to Beijing. With the withdrawal of U.S. forces from Afghanistan and the possible knock-on effects of Western sanctions against Russia throughout Central Asia, military pressure on China's western borders might soon increase, which could then force Beijing to shift away from the sea and back to the land.

* * *

(D) The world's attention is currently focused on Russia's invasion of Ukraine, but on the horizon, it is still China that looms as potentially the most important, as well as perhaps the most dangerous, rising power during the upcoming "Pacific Century." Some commentators have even argued that war between the United States and China might be inevitable.[8] Others do not agree. Building a constructive and lasting political relationship with a fast-rising China is one of the most important security challenges facing the United States today.

China is facing a monumental decision: to help Russia or not to help Russia? To assist Putin might further the PRC's land power interests, but it could also sideline China's transition to being one of the world's newest sea powers. If Xi decides to back Putin fully, Western sanctions, tariffs, and even a commercial blockade might be in China's near-term future. This could derail Beijing's hope of becoming perhaps the most important member of the twenty-first century global economy. It could also disrupt critical oil and food supplies, both of which China is now dependent on for its sheer survival.

The first step in carrying out any neo-Cold War strategy would be to force China and Russia to cooperate more closely with each other politically, commercially, and militarily. Coincidentally, this is already beginning to happen as a result of the Russian invasion of Ukraine. The more Moscow and Beijing are pushed together, however, the better the chance they will eventually split apart. As shown by the history of the Cold War, America's victory in a second Cold War would be assured. What will Xi Jinping do? Will China stay the course and become a sea power? Or will it turn back and become a land power again?

* * *

(E) From the height of the British Empire to the present day, sea powers have set the global order, and land powers have contested it. This dynamic is clearly still with us today. Xi must now decide whether to back Putin—the continental approach—or to become more deeply integrated into the

---

8 See Graham Allison, *Destined for War: Can America and China Escape Thucydide's Trap?* (New York: Houghton Mifflin Harcourt, 2018).

Anglo-American-led maritime global order through greater participation in multinational organizations seeking to uphold international legal norms. China's sea power shift could significantly strengthen the global system and, in so doing, better position the rapidly growing list of countries favoring the positive-sum maritime approach to await a change of heart by Moscow.

The PRC is going through sea power birthing pains right now. This situation will arguably get worse before it gets better. As this short history has sought to show, the 14 points that helped win the first Cold War against the USSR can be turned equally well against China. For example, a long-term strategy could be adopted to force China and Russia closer together, with the ultimate goal of increasing underlying Sino-Russian tensions. The strategic embargoes against Russia could then be linked with a "Russia differential" that would make any goods purchased from China much more dear, with the goal of creating a Sino-Russian split and then eventually a full break.

Although these critical Cold War events were often marginalized or overlooked entirely by Eurocentric historians, it was in China where the Cold War would ultimately be won or lost. The East-West pincer movement resulted in the destruction of the USSR and victory in the Cold War. But in today's world, China, not Russia, has arguably become the greatest potential threat to the world order. Putin's ongoing war against Ukraine is challenging the West. Will Xi Jinping back the continentalist Putin? Or will China eventually decide to throw in its hat on the side of the Anglo-American-led sea powers?

SELECTED BIBLIOGRAPHY

Allison, Graham, *Destined for War: Can America and China Escape Thucydide's Trap?* (New York: Houghton Mifflin Harcourt, 2018).

Barlow, Jeffrey G., *From HOT WAR to COLD: The U.S. Navy and National Security Affairs, 1945-1955* (Stanford, CA: Stanford University Press, 2009).

Beloff, Max, *Soviet Far Eastern Policy Since Yalta* (New York: Institute of Pacific Relations, 1950).

Black, Black, Ed., *The Seventy Great Battles of All Time* (London: Thames & Hudson, 2005).

Blechman, Barry M. and Berman, Robert P., *Guide to Far Eastern Navies* (Annapolis, MD: Naval Institute Press, 1978).

Bouchard, Joseph F., *Command in Crisis: Four Case Studies* (New York: Columbia University Press, 1991).

Campi, Alicia J., *The Political Relationship Between the United States and Outer Mongolia, 1915-1927: The Kalgan Consular Records* (Indiana University Dissertation, 1988), 202–203.

Chang, Gordan H., *Friends and Enemies: The United States, China, and the Soviet Union, 1948-1972* (Stanford, CA: Stanford University Press, 1990).

Chang, Jung and Halliday, Jon, *Mao: The Unknown Story* (New York: Alfred A, Knopf, 2005).

Chang, Pao-Min, *Sino-Vietnamese Territorial Dispute* (New York: Praeger, 1986).

Chen Jian, *Mao's China & the Cold War* (Chapel Hill, NC: The University of North Carolina Press, 2001).

Chen, King C., *China's War with Vietnam, 1979* (Stanford, CA: Hoover Institution Press, 1987).

Chiang Kai-shek, *China's Destiny* (New York: The MacMillan Company, 1947).

Christensen, Thomas J., *Useful Adversaries: Grand Strategy, Domestic Mobilization, and Sino-American Conflict, 1947-1958* (Princeton, NJ: Princeton University Press, 1996).

Chuprin, V. I., *"Voinnaya Mozh Podnebesnoi;Vooruzhenniye Sil KNR"* (Minsk: Harvest, 2007).

Cohen, Warren I., Ed., *New Frontiers in American-East Asian Relations* (New York: Columbia University Press, 1983).

Cole Bernard D., *The Great Wall at Sea* (Annapolis, MD: Naval Institute Press, 2001).

Daugherty, Leo J., III, *The Marine Corps and the State Department: Enduring Partners in United States Foreign Policy, 1798-2007* (Jefferson, NC: Macfarland & Company Inc. Publishers, 2009).

Day, Alan J., Ed., *Border and Territorial Disputes*, Keesings Reference Publication (Detroit: Gale Research Co., 1982).

Dayer, Roberta Allbert, *Bankers and Diplomats in China 1917-1925 The Anglo-American Relationship* (London: Frank Cass and Co., 1981).

Degras, Jane, *Soviet Documents on Foreign Policy. Volume 2, 1925-1932* (New York: Oxford University Press, 1952).

Dikötter, Frank, *Mao's Great Famine: The History of China's Most Devastating Catastrophe, 1958-1962* (New York: Walker & Co., 2010).

Doolin, Dennis J., *Territorial Claims in the Sino-Soviet Conflict* (Hoover Institution Studies: 7, 1965).

Dornan, James, *Chinese War Machine* (New York: Crescent, 1979).

Dulles, Foster Rhea, *American Policy Toward Communist China, 1949-1969* (New York: Thomas Y. Crowell Company, 1972).

Durkin, Michael F., *Naval Quarantine: A New Addition to the Role of Sea Power* (Maxwell Air Force Base, AL: Air University: Air War College, 1964).

Elleman, Bruce A., *Diplomacy and Deception: The Secret History of Sino-Soviet Diplomatic Relations, 1917-1927* (Armonk, NY: M.E. Sharpe, 1997).

Elleman, Bruce A., *Modern Chinese Warfare, 1795-1989* (London: Routledge Press, 2001).

Elleman, Bruce A., *Wilson and China: A Revised History of the Shandong Question* (Armonk, NY: M.E. Sharpe, 2002).

Elleman, Bruce A., *Moscow and the Emergence of Communist Power in China, 1925-30: The Nanchang Uprising and the Birth of the Red Army* (London: Routledge, 2009).

Elleman, Bruce A., *High Sea's Buffer: The Taiwan Patrol Force, 1950-1979* (Newport, RI: NWC Press, 2012).

Elleman, Bruce A. and Bell, Christopher, Eds., *Naval Mutinies of the Twentieth Century: An International Perspective* (London: Frank Cass, 2003).

Elleman, Bruce A. and Bussert, James, *People's Liberation Army Navy (PLAN) Combat Systems Technology, 1949-2010* (Annapolis: Naval Institute Press, 2011).

Elleman, Bruce A. and Kotkin, Stephen, Eds., *Manchurian Railways and the Opening of China, An International History* (Armonk NY: M.E. Sharpe, 2010).

Elleman, Bruce A. and Paine, S.C.M., Eds., *Naval Blockades and Seapower: Strategies and Counter-Strategies, 1805-2005* (London: Routledge Press, 2006).

Elleman, Bruce A. and Paine, S.C.M., *Modern China: Continuity and Change 1644 to the Present* (Boston: Prentice-Hall, 2010).

Elleman, Bruce A. and Paine, S.C.M., Eds., *Naval Power and Expeditionary Warfare: Peripheral Campaigns and New Theatres of Naval Warfare* (London: Routledge Press, 2011).

Elliott, David W. P., Ed., *The Third Indochina Conflict* (Boulder, CO: Westview Press, 1981).

Eudin, Xenia Joukoff and North, Robert C., *Soviet Russia and the East, 1920-1927* (Stanford, CA: Stanford University Press, 1957).

Friedman, Norman, *Naval Institute Guide to World Naval Weapons Systems, 1997-1998* (Annapolis MD: USNI Press, 1997).

Garthoff, Raymond L., Ed., *Sino-Soviet Military Relations* (New York: Frederick A Praeger, 1966).

Garver, John W., *China's Decision for Rapprochement with the United States, 1968-1971* (Boulder, CO: Westview Press, 1982).

Gittings, John, *The Role of the Chinese Army* (New York: Oxford University Press, 1967).

Goodspeed, M. Hill, *U.S. Navy: A Complete History* (Washington, DC: Naval Historical Foundation, 2003).

Hinton, Harold C., *China's Turbulent Quest* (New York: The Macmillan Company, 1972).

Hood, Steven J., *Dragons Entangled: Indochina and the China-Vietnam War* (Armonk, NY: M.E. Sharpe, 1992).

Hsü, Immanuel C.Y., *The Rise of Modern China* (New York: Oxford University Press, 1990).

Hyland, William, *The Cold War is Over* (New York: Random House, 1990).

Iriye, Akira, *After Imperialism, The Search for a New Order in the Far East, 1921-1931* (Cambridge, MA: Harvard University Press, 1965)

Kaplan, Brad, "China's Navy Today: Storm Clouds on the Horizon . . . or Paper Tiger?" *Sea Power*, December 1999.

Khrushchev, Nikita Sergeevich and Khrushchev, Sergei, *Memoirs of Nikita Khrushchev: Statesman, 1953-1964* (College Park: Penn State Press, 2007).

Kierman, Frank A., Jr. and Fairbank, Eds., *Chinese Ways of Warfare* (Cambridge, MA: Harvard University Press, 1974).

Kissinger, Henry, *White House Years* (Boston: Little, Brown and Company, 1979).

Kondapalli Srikanth, *China's Naval Power* (New Delhi: Knowledge World, 2001).

Levine, Steven I., *Anvil of Victory: The Communist Revolution in Manchuria, 1945-1948* (New York: Columbia University Press, 1987)

Lewis, John Wilson and Xue, Litai, *China's Strategic Seapower* (Stanford, CA: Stanford University Press, 1994).

Li, Xiaobing, *A History of the Modern Chinese Army* (Lexington, KY: The University of Kentucky, 2007).

Liu, Ta Jen, *U.S.-China Relations, 1784-1992* (Lanham, MD: University Press of America, 1997).

Lu Ch'iu-wen, *Chung-e Wai-meng Chiao-she Shih-mo* (The Ins and Outs of Sino-Russian Negotiations on Outer Mongolia) (Taipei, Taiwan: Cheng-wen Publishing Company, 1976).

Lüthi, Lorenz M., *The Sino-Soviet Split: Cold War in the Communist World* (Princeton. NJ: Princeton University Press, 2008).

Mahan, Alfred Thayer, *The Influence of Sea Power upon History 1660–1783* (1890; repr. New York: Wang and Hill, 1957).

Marolda, Edward J., *The U.S. Navy and the Chinese Civil War, 1945-1952* (Ph.D. Dissertation, The George Washington University, 1990).

Morris, Stephen J., *Why Vietnam Invaded Cambodia: Political Culture and the Causes of War* (Stanford, CA: Stanford University Press, 1999).

Muller, David, *China as a Maritime Power* (Boulder, CO: Westview Press, 1983).

O'Dowd, Edward C., *Chinese Military Strategy in the Third Indochina War: The Last Maoist War* (London: Routledge Press, 2007).

Okorokov, Alexander, *CCCP v Borbe za Mirovoe Gospodstvo* (Moscow: Eksmo, 2009).

Paine, S.C.M. *The Wars for Asia, 1911–1949* (New York: Cambridge University Press, 2012).

Powell, Ralph L., *The Rise of Chinese Military Power, 1895-1912* (Princeton, NJ: Princeton University Press, 1955).

Ray, Hemen, *China's Vietnam War* (New Delhi: Radiant Publishers, 1983).

Ross, Robert S., *The Indochina Tangle* (New York: Columbia University Press, 1988).

Rupen, Robert, *How Mongolia is Really Ruled: A Political History of the Mongolian People's Republic 1900-1978* (Stanford, CA: Stanford University Press, 1979).

Ryan, Mark A., Finkelstein, David M., and McDevitt, Michael A., *Chinese Warfighting: The PLA Experience Since 1949* (Armonk, NY: M.E. Sharpe, 2003).

Schell, Orville, *Mandate of Heaven* (New York: Simon & Schuster, 1994).

Snell, John L., Ed., *The Meaning of Yalta* (Baton Rouge: Louisiana State University Press, 1956).

Solomon, Richard H. and Kosaka, Masataka, Eds., *The Soviet Far East Military Buildup* (Dover, MA: Auburn House Publishing Company, 1986).

Stettinius, Edward R., Jr., *Roosevelt and the Russians* (Garden City, NY: Doubleday & Company, Inc., 1949).

Stremski, Richard, *Britain's China Policy, 1920-1928,* (University of Wisconsin Dissertation, 1968).

Sun Yat-sen, *The Vital Problems of China* (Taipei: China Cultural Service, 1953 reprint).

Swanson, Bruce, *Eighth Voyage of the Dragon: A History of China's Quest for Seapower* (Annapolis, MD: Naval Institute Press, 1982).

Tang, Peter S.H., *Russian and Soviet Policy in Manchuria and Outer Mongolia 1911-1932* (Durham, NC: Duke University Press, 1959).

Thaku, Ramesh and Thayer, Carlyle, *Soviet Relations with India and Vietnam* (New York: St. Martin's Press, 1992).

Vilenskii, Vladimir, *Kitai i Sovetskaia Rossiia (China and Soviet Russia)* (Moscow: Gosudarstvennoe izdatel'stvo, 1919).

Vincent, John Carter, *The Extraterritorial System in China* (Cambridge, MA: Harvard University Press, 1970).

Wilson, John, *China's Strategic Seapower* (Stanford, CA: Stanford University Press, 1994).

Wright, Richard N.J., *The Chinese Steam Navy, 1862-1945* (London: Chatham Publishing, 2000).

Wu, Hsiang-hsiang, *E-ti Ch'in-lueh Chung-kuo Shih* (A History of Imperial Russia's Invasion of China) (Taipei, Taiwan: Cheng Chung Book Company, 1954).

Wu, Shicun and Zou Keyuan, Eds., *Arbitration Concerning the South China Sea: Philippines versus China* (Surrey: Ashgate, 2016).

Young, Marilyn, *The Vietnam Wars, 1945-1990* (New York: HarperCollins, 1991).

Yu, Peter Kien-hong, *The Four Archipelagoes in the South China Sea* (Taipei: Council for Advanced Policy Studies, 1991).

ABOUT THE AUTHOR

Bruce A. Elleman was born in Columbus, Ohio, in 1959. He received the BA from UC Berkeley in 1982, the MA in 1984, a master of philosophy degree in 1987, an East Asian Certificate in 1988, and his PhD in 1993 at Columbia University. In addition, he completed a master of sciences degree at the London School of Economics in 1985 and a master of arts in national security and strategic studies (with distinction) at the Naval War College, Newport, Rhode Island, in 2004.

Elleman's dissertation research on Sino-Soviet diplomatic relations was conducted in Russia (1988–1989), the People's Republic of China (1990–1991), Taiwan (1991–1992), and Japan (1992–1993). Dr. Elleman was a Title VIII Fellow, Hoover Institution, Stanford University, 1993–1994, and National Fellow, Hoover Institution, Stanford University, 1994–1995. Elleman then taught in the history department at Texas Christian University, eventually receiving tenure there. He spent the 1998 calendar year at International Christian University, Tokyo, as a visiting fellow. In 2000, Dr. Elleman moved to the Center for Naval Warfare Studies at the U.S. Naval War College. In 2002–2003, he was a research fellow at the Slavic Research Center, Hokkaido University, and the recipient of a Social Science Research Council grant for advanced research on Japan. In 2013, he was made the William V. Pratt Professor of International History at the U.S. Naval War College.

Elleman is the author of 36 books. His dissertation was published as *Diplomacy and Deception: The Secret History of Sino-Soviet Diplomatic Relations, 1917–1927* (Armonk, N.Y.: M. E. Sharpe, 1997). He coedited with Stephen Kotkin *Mongolia in the Twentieth Century: Landlocked Cosmopolitan* (Armonk, N.Y.: M.E. Sharpe, 1999). His other books include *Modern Chinese Warfare, 1795–1989* (London: Routledge, 2001, translated into Chinese); *Wilson and China: A Revised History of the 1919 Shandong Question* (Armonk, N.Y.: M.E. Sharpe, 2002); *Naval Mutinies of the Twentieth Century: An International Perspective*, coedited with Christopher Bell (London: Frank Cass, 2003, translated into Czech); *Japanese-American Civilian Prisoner Exchanges and Detention Camps, 1941–45* (London: Routledge, 2006); *Naval Blockade and Seapower: Strategies and*

Counter-Strategies, 1805–2005, coedited with S. C. M. Paine (London: Routledge, 2006); *Waves of Hope: The U.S. Navy's Response to the Tsunami in Northern Indonesia.* Newport Paper 28 (Newport, R.I.: Naval War College Press, 2007); *Naval Coalition Warfare: From the Napoleonic War to Operation Iraqi Freedom*, coedited with S. C. M. Paine (London: Routledge, 2008); *Moscow and the Emergence of Communist Power in China, 1925-30: The Nanchang Uprising and the Birth of the Red Army*(London: Routledge, 2009); *Manchurian Railways and the Opening of China: An International History*, coedited with Stephen Kotkin (Armonk NY: M.E. Sharpe Northeast Asia Series, 2010); *Nineteen Gun Salute: Case Studies of Operational, Strategic, and Diplomatic Naval Leadership during the 20th and Early 21st Centuries*, coedited with John B. Hattendorf (Newport: NWC Press, 2010); *Piracy and Maritime Crime: Historical and Modern Case Studies*, coedited with Andrew Forbes and David Rosenberg (Newport: NWC Press, Newport Paper 35, 2010); *Modern China: Continuity and Change 1644 to the Present*, coauthored with S. C. M. Paine (Prentice-Hall, 2010); *Naval Power and Expeditionary Wars: Peripheral Campaigns and New Theatres of Naval Warfare*, coedited with S. C. M. Paine (London: Routledge, 2011); *People's Liberation Army Navy (PLAN) Combat Systems Technology 1949-2010*, coauthored witht Jim Bussert (Annapolis, MD: Naval Institute Press, 2011); *China as a Sea Power, 1127-1368: A Preliminary Survey of the Maritime Expansion and Naval Exploits of the Chinese People During the Southern Sung and Yuan Periods*, Unpublished manuscript by Professor Jung-pang Lo, edited, and with commentary, by Bruce A. Elleman, (Singapore: National University of Singapore Press, and Hong Kong: University of Hong Kong Press, 2012); *High Sea's Buffer: The Taiwan Patrol Force, 1950-1979* (NWC Press, 2012);); *Beijing's Power and China's Borders: Twenty Neighbors in Asia*, coedited by Bruce Elleman, Stephen Kotkin, and Clive Schofield (Armonk, NY: M.E. Sharpe, 2013); *Commerce Raiding: Historical Case Studies, 1755-2009*, edited, with S. C. M. Paine (Newport, RI: NWC Press, 2013); *Taiwan Straits: Crisis in Asia and the Role of the U.S. Navy* (forthcoming, 2015), *International Competition in China: 1899-1991: The Rise, Fall, and Restoration of the Open Door Policy* (London: Routledge, 2015); *Navies and Soft Power: Historical Case Studies of Naval Power and the Nonuse of Military Force*, edited, with S. C. M. Paine (Newport, RI: NWC Press, 2015); *China's Naval Operations in the South China Sea: Evaluating Legal, Strategic and Military Factors* (Folkestone: Renaissance Press, 2018); and *Seaborne Perils: Piracy, Maritime Crime, and Naval Terrorism in Africa, South Asia, and Southeast Asia* (New York: Rowman & Littlefield, 2018); *Modern China: Continuity and Change 1644 to the Present*, Second Edition, coauthored with S. C. M. Paine (Prentice-Hall, 2019); *Taiwan's Offshore Islands: Pathway or Barrier?* (Newport, RI: NWC Press, 2019); *The Making of the Modern Chinese Navy: Special Historical Characteristics* (London: Anthem Press, 2019); *International Rivalry and Secret Diplomacy in East Asia, 1896-1950* (London: Routledge, 2019);

A History of the Modern Chinese Navy, 1840-2020 (London: Routledge/Curzon Press, 2021); *Taiwan Straits Standoff: 70 Years of PRC-Taiwan Cross-Strait Tensions* (London: Anthem Press, 2022); and *Principles of Maritime Power* (Lanham, MD: Rowman & Littlefield, 2022); *Empire in the Western Ocean: Sea Power and the Early Ming Navy, 1355-1449*, Lo Jung-Pang, coedited with Richard J. Smith and Geoff Wade (Hong Kong: Chinese University of Hong Kong Press, 2023); *The United States Navy's Pivot to Asia: The Origins of "A Cooperative Strategy for Twenty-First Century Seapower"* (London: Routledge Press, 2023); *The Impact of Coincidence in Modern American, British, and Asian History: Twenty-One Unusual Historical Events* (London: Anthem Press, 2023).

Several of Elleman's books have been translated into foreign languages, including a Chinese translation of *Modern Chinese Warfare* as *Jindai Zhongguo de junshi yu zhanzheng* (Taipei: Elite Press, 2002), and a Czech translation of *Naval Mutinies of the Twentieth Century: An International Perspective* as *Námořní vzpoury ve dvacátém století: mezinárodní souvislosti* (Prague: BBart, 2004).

INDEX

Printed in the USA
CPSIA information can be obtained
at www.ICGtesting.com
JSHW020745251024
72409JS00001B/8

9 781839 992278